S0-DLP-186

Ukrainian Classics in Translation

Edited by George S. N. Luckyj, University of Toronto

No. 3

Ukrainian Classics in Translation

Mykola Kulish

Sonata Pathetique

Translated from Ukrainian
by
George S. N. and Moira Luckyj

With Introduction
by
Ralph Lindheim
University of Toronto

1975

Ukrainian Academic Press

Copyright © 1975 Ukrainian Academic Press
All Rights Reserved
Printed in the United States of America

Library of Congress Card Number 73-91177
International Standard Book Number 0-87287-092-8

UKRAINIAN ACADEMIC PRESS
A Division of
Libraries Unlimited, Inc.
P.O. Box 263
Littleton, Colorado 80120

Cover design by M. Levytsky

Library of Congress Cataloging in Publication Data

Kulish, Mykola Hurovych, 1892-1937.
    Sonata pathetique.

    (Ukrainian classics in translation ; 3)
    Translation of Patetychna sonata.
    1. Ukraine—History—Revolution, 1917-1921—
Drama. I. Title. II. Series.
PG3948.K855P313   891.7'9'23   73-91177
ISBN 0-87287-092-8

TABLE OF CONTENTS

The publisher wishes to acknowledge
the assistance provided by
Ukrainian Research Foundation, Inc.,
Denver, Colorado.

INTRODUCTION

Mykola Kulish's *Sonata Pathetique* is as powerful, complex, and unconventional as the Beethoven sonata which gives the play its title and which is heard throughout its seven acts. Nevertheless, at first glance the play seems a typical early Soviet epic drama about revolution and civil war. Set in Ukraine and employing a large cast of characters, the play depicts the events of the years 1917-18, when the sleepy life of a small provincial town is disrupted by massive discontent with the Russian government, by the resurgence of dormant Ukrainian nationalism, and by the subversive activity of Bolshevik agitators. Soon the town divides into social and ideological camps, and the tension generated in this seething cauldron explodes in civil war, an armed struggle for power characterized by bloody skirmishes and vicious reprisals, heroic self-sacrifice and sordid betrayal. With the victory of the Red partisans, a victory which is not, however, portrayed as a conclusive triumph, the play ends on a conventional note, optimistically predicting the bright future of Ukraine under Bolshevik rule.

Despite the standard formulas, Kulish's play towers above the other Soviet historical epics written in the 1920's and '30's because of the brilliance of its technique and the integrity with which it explores the central issues of revolution and nationalism. Even when compared with the better works of the genre—for example, Mikhail Bulgakov's *The Days of the Turbins—Sonata Pathetique*'s excellence gleams brightly. Unlike Bulgakov's competent but vastly overrated play, which rests squarely on an old-fashioned naturalistic foundation, Kulish's drama is an unabashedly melodramatic, theatrical spectacle combining in an original manner the most effective features of Symbolist and Expressionist drama, a rich verbal texture, and a fragmented episodic structure. Besides the intriguing modernism of its style the scope of *Sonata Pathetique* is broader and more complex, treating the historical events with greater sympathy and understanding. Bulgakov, on the one hand, concentrates his

7

attention upon the Turbins—that decent, sensitive, cultured family whose day is over—abstains from presenting the Bolshevik point of view, and in a few brief strokes sketches the nationalists as coarse, peasant bandits more interested in sack and pillage than in national liberation; Kulish, however, brings to life all the antagonists of his play—the adherents of revolution, counterrevolution, and nationalism—and depicts extensively and honestly their emotions, their ideas, and their tragic failure to realize their deepest aspirations.

But to emphasize disproportionately either the modernistic style or the subject matter of *Sonata Pathetique* fails to isolate what is truly impressive, significant, and relevant about this play. Technical virtuosity and theatricality alone do not guarantee dramatic excellence or the survival of any play. And is there today a more hackneyed topic than revolution, especially revolution with nationalistic overtones? Popular culture glamorizes revolution, newspapers chart its violent course in many lands, and sociologists, political scientists, philosophers, and theologians speculate endlessly upon its national and international sources and consequences. Those marked as the revolution's first targets package it for financial gain (Castro jackets and commissar coats have long been fashionable), and those farthest removed from the reality of revolution tend to idealize it and assert its necessity (on many campuses "the God that failed" has yet to "flunk out"). The idea of revolution hangs so heavily in the air that plays on this subject, though not on the sexual revolution, fail to arouse and stimulate audiences. Yet if neither the stylistic originality of Kulish's play nor its picture of revolutionary change in the recent past can or even should have a lasting impact on its viewers, the seamless fabric of both style and content in *Sonata Pathetique* projects an overwhelming experience of revolution that should impress and enlighten audiences everywhere and might even prove a revelation to us in the West who idealize revolution without having participated in anything more violent than a scrap with college administrators, politicians, and policemen. In the darkened theater we can feel, for a few hours at least, what it must be like to live at a critical stage of history when the traditional way of the world is questioned, when the old order, with all its assumptions, crumbles under the insistent pressure of different and divergent visions of man and society as these visions contend against the established view and among themselves for understanding, allegiance, and power.

With the same resonance and force of the explosive phrase beginning Beethoven's *Sonata Pathetique*, the opening notes of the play, in which the hero-narrator sets the place and the time of the action, startle us in the audience and propel us immediately into the situation that confronts the characters:

> Imagine, my friends, he started to say: 1) a street in an old provincial city, 2) a two-story building with a sign "the residence of Major-General Perotsky," 3) a revolutionary spring, 4) Easter night.

We are not asked to picture an ordinary, typical spring that momentarily warms the earth and temporarily brightens the overcast winter sky, and we are not invited to celebrate dutifully yet another Easter with its routine message of the cyclical flow of the seasons; instead, we are asked to imagine an Easter eve that falls in an extraordinary spring, an apocalyptic spring, in which light, heat, and all the vital, creative forces of nature will attack the dark, the cold, and all the stifling, destructive powers of winter so vigorously that the real promise of Easter, the final triumph of life over death, will at last be realized. These intoxicating expectations are strengthened in the first act, for this sleepy town is not gently roused from hibernation but is shaken and jolted awake as the inhabitants become aware of the sweeping changes that have just occurred in the capitals of Russia and Ukraine, the February Revolution in Petrograd and the formation of the Rada in Kiev. Their long-smoldering discontent with everyone and everything that had sustained the old, bankrupt order and that was continuing inertly to uphold it at the moment of its collapse is rekindled by the propaganda of Bolshevik agents, who have recently arrived in the town, and fanned by the bitter hatred of returning veterans (like Ovram), who were forced to fight on the Russian side in World War I and were mutilated in this unpopular war.

At first the desire for change gives birth to just a few minor gestures of rebellion—the refusal of the local prostitute Zinka to receive her usual customers and the strikes of the factory workers—but behind these irritating but harmless acts looms the real threat of greater turbulence, a threat based on the intense factional disputes among the respected and powerful leaders of the community, the members of the intelligentsia and the wealthy manufacturers and property owners. No single ideological cause lacks staunch defenders. The Perotsky family supports the Russians; the Stupay-Stupanenko family, the Ukrainian nationalists; and the young students Ilko Yuha and

Luka, the cause of international revolution. Moreover, within each faction friction already exists or is latent. Major Perotsky and his son Georges remain loyal to the Imperial Russian government, the empire that no longer exists but that they would gladly restore; André Perotsky supports the Provisional Government formed after the February Revolution; Maryna and her father fail to agree on either the tactics or the goals of nationalism; and Ilko and Luka strain their friendship by quarreling about the revolutionary ends to which the Bolsheviks should dedicate themselves.

The bleak prospect of anarchy, however, fails to dampen the spirits of the characters and to cure their spring fever, for even this portent is a sign of life, signaling the lifting of the oppressive yoke of the old order. The young who had been held back from positions of responsibility and power by their elders, the proletarians who had been mercilessly exploited by the middle classes, the nationalists who had been muzzled by chauvinistic Russians and their Ukrainian quislings—all hail their liberation from the stifling forces that had drained them of their strength and repressed their aspirations as well as those of their country. Summing up the sentiments of so many of his countrymen, Stupay writes in his chronicle, "A month ago I could not sleep at night, thinking all the time that the night was as big as Russia and Russia as big as the night and nothing was heard of our Ukraine. But today I read the declaration of our Central Rada: To the Ukrainian people, the people of peasants, workers and all toilers. . . . After one month—what a change. I bless the revolution!" (I, ix). Together with the old teacher all "bless" the external changes wrought by the revolution but also the more significant and radical transformation of consciousness produced by the flash floods of this revolutionary spring. Through the cracks of the disintegrating dykes beyond the town the waters surge through the streets, washing up into the hearts and minds of the characters and liberating the energy within them that had so long been denied expression. No longer do they view their surroundings as familiar, dull, and empty. Now, as the imagery of the play indicates, they see their world and themselves as vibrant, dynamic, active. The sounds of Beethoven's music burst through the silence of "the Russian night" and quicken the pulse of so many of the characters who translate the rhythms, moods, and themes of the sonata's movements into images of great power and motion (Cossacks on horses sweeping over the steppes), images of force and intensity (a fugue of Easter bells), and images of breathtaking beauty:

> Maryna is playing the same *Sonata Pathetique*, but today I can't hear the starry *grave* or the brilliant *allegro*, but the gay *adagio cantabile* like flowers in the sun. As usual, I can visualize a limitless steppe and above, in the Argonaut boat, she floats, with her left eyebrow raised, her eyes deep blue, and there are flowers and dew on the oars. (II, i)

The color symbolism of the play emphasizes the fierce interplay of the primary colors—the clash of red against yellow and blue as well as their mutual struggle with blackness. Other striking figurative clusters include the images of unrestricted movement (such as the seagull soaring over Ukraine, the flags waving, and the banners flying); the images of the penetration of darkness and stillness by the Ukrainian stars, the Bolshevik wind, and the inextinguishable pipes of counterrevolution; and the images of might (such as the hetman's mace, the Napoleonic tricorn, and the locomotive of the revolution). All of these suggest that with the flooding of the land the characters find themselves in a strange world full of glorious music, rich color, and grand spectacle, a world as magical as Prospero's island in *The Tempest*. And they see themselves as the noble men and women of strength and spirit required to pioneer this "brave new world."

The pulsating currents of this spring invigorate the young and rejuvenate the old. All talk, gesture, and move energetically as, dashing madly from place to place, they parade, organize, proselytize, intrigue, and fight. The Bolsheviks—depicted iconographically as vigorous automatons who sacrifice to their cause all mundane desires for security, comfort, and pleasure, and all personal feelings of love and friendship—display the strongest movements and the most forceful gestures (Luka flexing his muscles in V, i). And their images for the revolution portray it conventionally as an overwhelming natural and mechanical force—the wind and the locomotive. The nationalists, however, are far from quiescent: they, too, express their newly acquired sense of power in words as insolent and bold as their thoughts and deeds. Stupay-Stupanenko taunts his Russian landlord and spits out his defiance of the disintegrating empire that Perotsky represents, "Holy Russia, you daughter of a bitch, we'll kick your big fat backside now" (I, xiii). While he rages, his daughter Maryna plans daring action against both Russia and Poland and searches for a brave knight who will break the stranglehold, the "rusty locks" (II, iii), that these countries have put on Ukraine. In addition to galvanizing them physically, the unleashed energy also fires their cold souls. Their renewed capacity to dream—and almost everyone in the play begins to dream again—points most strikingly to their spiritual regeneration. Some dream of their country's glorious past, recent and distant: Perotsky nostalgically recalls the fragrant, peaceful Easter of 1913 when the Russian Empire was still intact, while Stupay has visions of the autonomous Cossack Ukraine of the seventeenth century; others dream of Ukraine as a powerful, modern state, fully independent (Maryna) or linked with Russia in a union governed by the dictatorship of the proletariat (Luka) or by a dictatorial board of Napoleonic supermen (André); and still others, whose yearnings are more private than public, more personal than social, dream of love and of the other blessings that freedom will soon bring lyrically and idealistically (Ilko), crudely and erotically (Georges), prosaically and desperately (Zinka and Ovram's wife, Nastia).

Exhilarated by the discovery of their physical and spiritual power, the characters refuse to play their traditional roles as ordinary citizens of an insignificant, provincial town and to adhere to long established customs and manners. As they become aware of their vast potential, they inflate their image of themselves to heroic proportions and imagine themselves as titans representing man in general or Ukraine or Russia in particular, as defenders of the ennobling ideals of the past, as champions of love, justice, equality, the national spirit, etc. Whereas some explicitly identify themselves with mythological and historical heroes—Jason and the Argonauts, Joan of Arc, Petrarch, Napoleon, and the illustrious poets and military leaders of Ukraine, Shevchenko, Bohdan, Doroshenko, Mazepa, Kalnysh, and Honta, are mentioned—the actions of all the characters reveal implicitly their heroic posture, their confidence that their strength and will are sufficient to direct the future course of their personal lives, their countries, and history itself towards objectives that are desirable, creative, and moral. Both Zinka and Ilko reject passivity and go out in search of the ideal, she onto the streets to find a true lover and he to Maryna's apartment to deliver his declaration of love, the last in a long series of torn, discarded letters. Hamar, with the assistance of Luka, begins to work openly among the workers and to organize their protests. Stupay initiates his campaign to make his fellow countrymen more aware and proud of their own culture. Maryna rejects Ilko and selects André as the chivalric champion to realize her scheme for the liberation of Ukraine. And even Major Perotsky marshals his fading powers and memories to defend the empire under attack.

In the same way that the radical transformation of consciousness is amplified by the imagery of the play, the resurgence of physical and spiritual energy, which is also central to the experience of revolution that *Sonata Pathetique* projects, is embodied in the other striking stylistic feature of the play, its rhythmic dynamism. No audience can fail to sense that in the world of the play the pace of the characters' lives is not smooth, even, regular. To the normal tempo of everyday life, suggested by the metronomic beat of the clock in the Perotsky apartment and the water dripping from the basement ceiling, are juxtaposed the tempi of revolutionary life when time speeds up or slows down but never moves regularly. The brisk tempo is built up, of course, by the energetic movements of the characters but it is even more powerfully conveyed by the rapid scene changes within the one setting used in the play—the inside and outside of the large house where all the characters live or meet and where they test their emotions and ideas. Within this vast playing space the action does not sweep evenly from top to bottom or side to side and does not flow logically from interior to exterior, but moves spasmodically, hopscotching floors, leaping diagonally from stage right to stage left, surging frantically and, at times, unexpectedly from house to street and back again. In contrast to these abrupt, harsh scenic shifts stand intense moments of subjective reflection and reverie when the fast tempo is arrested and the characters have time to voice their hopes, expectations, and dreams or when the action is momentarily retarded, as on the night of the Bolshevik seizure of power, and the characters (Ilko in this instance) enter into a dream world:

> I feel strange: I stand on guard, but all around me music flows. A yellowish streak of light flashes somewhere (Maryna lifts the edge of the tapestry in the window) and disappears with a blue afterglow. It is swept away by the wind and the music of the *Pathetique* (she moves away from the window and plays the *grave*). Behind the bass chords horses' hooves can be heard. Someone is making a fire. A horse is racing through the dark steppe. That is me, racing on a horse into the land of eternal love! Behind the black horizon, near the blue window she is waiting for me, looking out for me. (Now Maryna once again uncovers the window and looks out. She is going downstairs to meet me.) She is stretching out her hands, her left eyebrow is a little

raised and her eyes are smiling. (She looks at me in my sleep.) We are engulfed by the music of the *rondo*. It is a silvery serpentine melody. At the same time I can feel the wind and see the night. "The sun doesn't love the earth as much as I love you," I want to say to Maryna, but I can not. She, as it were, moves away, floats away. The serpentine melody is broken and is carried away by the wind. She seems to be in a boat. I see the mast, the billowing sail, the taut ropes. Instead of the *rondo* I hear once more the *grave*. Maryna stands under the sail.

    —Is this the Argo?, I ask.
    —This is an old Zaporozhian boat, she answers.
    —Cossack boats had no sails, I mention.
    —This is not a sail!

I look and see a flag, a yellow and blue one. We sail off. Luka comes to meet us. Bent over, he carries a red banner on his back. For some reason it is as round as the moon. I remember that I left my guard post, that to him I am a traitor. I am overcome with shame, restlessness and fear.

(IV, vi)

In these interludes the characters glide across the stage like dancers, render their gestures in slow motion, and express themselves in operatic arias and ensembles.

It may be argued that the tempi of the play, inspired no doubt by Beethoven's music, are fairly conventional, demanded by the very genre of the work. Yet upon these contrasting tempi necessitated by the melodramatic action and the episodic structure Kulish imposes a distinctive rhythm to make more palpable the telescoping of time, to suggest still another aspect of the revolutionary experience, and to express his own vision of this world of energy and its devastating effects on the characters. Throughout *Sonata Pathetique* this rhythm is heard (faintly in the first two acts, clearly articulated in the middle acts) and it dominates the final acts, driving the play to its shattering conclusion.

Act III, in its entirety, exhibits fully the fast tempo of the play as well as the rhythmic impulse which adds color, depth, and meaning to the swift pace. Again it is the visual flow of the action that is significant as it darts from Stupay and Luka on the street with the crowd, to Major Perotsky on his balcony, to Maryna and André on her balcony, and finally to Georges on the roof. Almost all the different playing areas on the stage are illuminated and allowed to sprawl together in a chaotic jumble. The scenic cuts here and for the rest of the play are not just swift and abrupt but brutally jagged, giving the impression of energy too intense to be manipulated, too powerful to be tamed.

How the rhythm of the play progressively dominates the slow movements of *Sonata Pathetique* is revealed by comparing two scenes in which Maryna relates her dream of the liberation of Ukraine. In the second act she reveals her hopes for the future to André, intending to delight and seduce with her vision's lyric charm and beauty the officer already enchanted by her beauty and charismatic personality:

> Maryna: And guess what I dream about when I listen to this music?
> André: Your father?
> Maryna: Something wonderful and unintelligible. Vision, dream and reality all merge into one. The country is dark and wild, so oppressed that it has even forgotten its history and doesn't know what will happen to it tomorrow. The dream: Two rusty locks hang on a gate, one with a white and the other with a two-headed eagle. The past and the future are locked. There is a lonely girl in this dark country. She dreams and waits. Do you know for whom?
> André: For whom?
> Maryna: A knight who loves Ukrainian stars.
> André: Really?
> Maryna: Day after day, night after night I wait for him to come and break these locks and open the gate. . . .
> André: For the girl?
> Maryna: For the girl and for the country.
>
> (II, iii)

In the fifth act, however, her dream state and the dream itself are of a different order and intensity. Excited by the signal of the imminent counterattack by the nationalist partisans against the Bolsheviks, she faces her father, who has lost faith in the success of the nationalist cause, and attempts to revive his fallen spirits:

> The pipe of counterrevolution. Today! (*She rapturously plays some chords from the* Sonata Pathetique.) Do you hear, father? Do you hear, my gray mustache, how our Cossacks are racing from the neighboring villages? We are ready! (*She gets up as if in ecstasy.*) Omphalos, omphalos! The pipes have been lit! (*She dances.*) No matter how strong the wind from the north it won't blow out the fire. No, it will intensify it. Blow until the sparks fly (*she strikes the keyboard*)! Omphalos! Light your pipes so that the smoke spreads across the steppe and into the heavens. Smoke until the sky is dense with it, until God sends you an angel who, as in a folktale, will ask you: "What do you want, you Cossacks who have smoked so much?" We want our own state under this flag. (*With her hair streaming*

15

across her back she brings out the flag she has been hiding and unfolds it.) Under this flag!

(V, iii)

Again Maryna wants to manipulate her listener only to find that she cannot control herself. Seized by the spirit of prophecy and cast into a trance, she gives voice not to an artfully designed, restrained fantasy, but to an ecstatic vision whose frenzied language, ferocious imagery, and throbbing incantational beat testify to the hallucinatory nature of her present dream, as shrill, hysterical, and febrile as the former had been calm, confident, and healthy. The rhythm that intimates Maryna's derangement, a temporary insanity that becomes permanent in the final act, reverberates in the later dreams of the other characters, in the frantic suggestion of pastoral retreat that André flings out at the end of the fourth act and that Maryna develops in the final scene, and in the last dream of Major Perotsky: "Russia was like a deserted field with a stove and an icon in the middle. Then Stupay comes and sits on the stove. What arrogance!" (IV, ix). In all these examples the rhythm indicates that the spiritual energy that had stimulated all of them to dream in the first place escapes from their control and develops so unnaturally that it poisons their minds and perverts their pure, noble visions into desperate escapist rhapsodies and grotesque nightmares.

The first soundings of this rhythm and its gradual amplification, suggesting that the people in this town are gradually overwhelmed by the energy that had liberated and activated them, is connected with the characters' progressive realization of the inaccessibility of their goals. Reality, even in a revolutionary situation, proves a recalcitrant medium that either fails to fulfill the expectations of its creatures or contradicts them mockingly. Those with the most worthy of personal goals are disappointed in their quests: all the men Zinka encounters do not meet her requirements or refuse to respond to her offer of herself, and Ilko is rejected by the only woman he loves. Nor can those pursuing more public goals, the creation of a new social and political order, accomplish their ends swiftly and efficiently by parading their strength—that is, merely by displaying the undeniable force of their ideas and of the personalities behind the ideas. Act three shows how each of this group of characters fails to receive from a populace divided in its loyalties and longings the support he needs for the immediate implementation of his ideological program: Stupay's

16

nationalism fails to move the workers, André's militaristic and imperialistic slogans excite the fashionable society ladies of the town but repel the common soldiers who must carry out his scheme, and Luka's Bolshevik propaganda arouses the most violent response, Georges's shot. Tarnished by the immediate opposition to their ideas, their heroic image of themselves is further sullied in the civil war initiated by the bullet from Georges's gun. In act four the nationalists are forced to acknowledge the error of their alliance with the Whites. Stupay is deeply disturbed by their ally's indifference to the question of cultural nationalism, and Maryna is visibly shaken by the revelation of the weakness of the White forces, their sudden collapse before the enemy has assumed the offensive. Naturally the Bolsheviks, with the tide in their favor, retain their poise and their faith in their own power to shake and change the world in a matter of days. "The world will be ours!" they assert in IV, vii, and in the next act Hamar and Luka plan the complete transformation of Ukrainian society:

> Hamar: Send a telegram to all revolutionary committees in the villages: "First task—sow more wheat." (*With a wide sweep of the hand*.) The steppes!

* * *

> Luka: Cable "Second: Organize the poor peasants. Tell the rich peasants that their houses won't be their own much longer. Third: On that side of the Dnieper there are deposits of coke. . . ."

(V, vii)

Yet they too have been wrenched by the active resistance to them. Formerly they had expected their opponents to preempt the revolution, to alter its direction and vitiate its force. They were prepared for "those who turn a revolution into an operetta or a liturgy and the class struggle into a parade" (II, i), but now they must face the reality of guerrilla warfare with foes too insidious to be dismissed lightly and too strong to be defeated easily.

Whatever the nature of his goal, each individual soon collides with major obstacles that abort or hinder his quest. Failure or frustration resulting from personal miscalculation or external interference drain him of confidence in himself and in the cause he supports. The heroic image finally shatters. This reversal, which all undergo, occurs first at the end of the second act when Ilko, distraught because of his unrequited love, proclaims the futility of all human action in a rank, decaying world:

17

What does it matter? Remember when you were still a little boy, you chased dreams on a hobbyhorse and sometimes fell off and cut your bare foot on a sharp broken glass till the piercing ache reached your heart? Remember how you fell off the hobbyhorse into some garbage? That's what it is now—garbage around you and you fell off your visionary horse. Is our world a garbage dump and do dreams rise from it like vapors? Yes, Luka, all our paths in this world are merely orbits. It doesn't matter which you take, you will go back where you started from—a hole. The difference is that when you are born you fall out of a hole, when you die you fall into a hole. That's all. Where shall I go? Try another orbit?

(II, v)

Though others do not bemoan their helplessness with such intense self-pity, many share Ilko's despair and come to see themselves as defenseless, vulnerable children. Quite early in the play Zinka suspects that she is an unfortunate child deserted by an indifferent God (I, xvi), and just before she betrays Georges to comrade Fate, she notes bitterly that she cannot offer her victim that which he so desperately wants—maternal love, comfort, and sustenance—since she herself had long searched for them in vain:

> *Zinka goes to open the door. Georges clings to the hem of her dress.*
> Georges: You are the Virgin Mary! You are my mother. Don't!
> Zinka (*struck by the word "mother"*): Say that again, will you?
> Georges: My mother.
> Zinka: Mother. Then you are my child. Don't cry! If you like I'll give you my breast to suck. No!... What kind of a mother am I... (*Angrily*) Be quiet! (*She opens the door.*)

(IV, xxx)

Lamenting the ideological barriers dividing Ukrainians who should be united by the desire to liberate their country, Stupay sees both the nationalists and the Bolsheviks as children abandoned to an unknown but unenviable fate when he notes, "It's a pity we're like orphans" (IV, iv). Finally, Maryna presents at the close of the play a pathetic picture of herself as a fragile, virginal child weakly pleading for mercy from the vicious forces that threaten her chastity and life: "Who will tell my old mother how I went to church for the passion, how I carried a candle home (*she pretends to carry a candle*) and you, the lusty wind (*she shields her imaginary candle from me and goes down*), want to blow out the candle of my life" (VII, iv).

At these moments the characters finally realize that they are not titans and the masters of history, but helpless children trapped in a world they cannot conquer and victimized by a historical process they cannot even comprehend, let alone manipulate according to their wills. That this perception is so sharp and so widely shared suggests that the sense of human insignificance and impotence is as central to the revolutionary experience Kulish is objectifying on stage as the sense of human power and creative potentiality that catapulted the characters into action at the opening of the play. Moreover, since this perception of impotence becomes ever more insistent in the play, gradually infecting all of the characters, its growth is directly proportional to that of the distinctive rhythmic impulse which sweeps over the world of the play and progressively determines its movement. This interrelationship, however, can be fully clarified only after a consideration of the various reactions of the characters to this gnawing awareness of their helplessness.

Of all the characters, those who seem to fall the hardest are Ilko and Stupay, the two men who want to civilize the Bolsheviks and to impress upon them the need for more daring, more idealistic, more revolutionary goals. Constantly lamenting, losing heart, questioning themselves and their causes, they seem to be utterly deflated by the discovery of their impotence. Yet the fluctuation of their allegiances and the inconsistency of their actions, which contradict the abstract principles they accept in theory, prove that they do not succumb to the perception of weakness but attempt to combat and overcome it. When Ilko offers his services to the Bolsheviks after Maryna has rejected him and when Stupay urges a new coalition between the nationalists and Bolsheviks, they modify their original commitments not because they have lost all hope for the realization of their cherished ideals, but because they are anxious to achieve them even more quickly and efficiently. When Ilko lies to save André from a Red firing squad and when Stupay offers Major Perotsky sanctuary from these same guns, they save the lives of men they consider dangerous enemies not because they are traitorous weaklings, but because their human feelings of love, compassion, and mercy are stronger than their desire for revenge or cold, revolutionary justice. Their intensely voiced admission of human insubstantiality neither warps their consciousness nor impairs their idealism, and both men strive to preserve higher ethical and cultural values from corruption and obliteration in the modern world of revolution. Ilko's love for poetry and visionary music cannot be shaken by freedom

19

fighters who try to convince him that action, not art, is required of all Ukrainian patriots. He responds with glad emotion when Maryna plays the piano on the night of the Bolshevik coup, so heartened is he to note that the voice of art cannot be quelled by the lurid atmosphere of the civil war: "Yes, she is playing. Let her boat, full of music, float in the middle of this anxious black night, disturbed by the wind" (IV, v). Stupay's reverence for the moral grandeur of the Zaporozhian Cossack tradition leads him to question the secretive, furtive maneuvers of Maryna and the unlimited power of her elite central committee to formulate policy and strategy, "Running again! I don't know whether I'm a Ukrainian of Zaporozhian descent or a horse. I don't understand anything. Some committee. There should be a military council, not a committee. That's not the way the Zaporozhians fought" (IV, iii). Thus, it is not surprising that at the most critical moments of their lives the intense despair that drives Ilko to the brink of suicide and Stupay to the attempt to divine the future mystically by means of Shevchenko's *Kobzar* does not penetrate their firmly rooted faith in human strength and will: Ilko does not kill himself, and Shevchenko's ringing line, "Bury me and then rise up," so restores Stupay that he dashes out to meet a cruelly unexpected death.

Unlike these two men, the other characters openly admit the fact of their impotence only at the very end of the play, when the pressures of the obstacles they encounter become intense enough to cloud their vision and dim their dreams. Betrayed by her lover and shocked by the death of her father, Maryna faces the final threat to her existence—Ilko's decision to turn her over to the Bolsheviks—and cracks under the strain. Her bright vision of Ukrainian independence, which had totally possessed and illuminated her being, now loses its intensity and shrinks in size, becoming a flickering candle whose puny flame struggles against extinction. Similarly, Luka has been jarred by betrayal and death, the discovery of the powerful, disciplined subversive group whose momentary triumph resulted in the execution of his comrade Ovram and the prostitute Zinka, who symbolized for him the downtrodden people the Bolsheviks had pledged to defend. His dream, too, diminishes in clarity and intensity to the point that it is almost obscured. The station toward which the revolutionary locomotive had hurled at full speed moves farther and farther into the future, and the journey, he informs Ilko, will not be as short, easy, and comfortable as he had once imagined, for "There are many temptations waiting for us on our way to our distant goal" (VII, iv). In effect, both Maryna and Luka confess that they are too weak to reach their objectives and that their main function is to defend the faith, to keep the candle burning or to hold the distant station in sight somewhere on the horizon, so that their followers will continue their work and perhaps realize their dreams. Though the confession of weakness occurs very late, the awareness of their incapacity to scale the heights they dreamed of conquering underlies many of their attitudes and actions in the critical central acts of *Sonata Pathetique*.

Luka and Maryna, who are ingeniously paired by Kulish and contrasted with Ilko and Stupay, seem unaffected by frustration and failure, to which they respond with renewed dedication to their objectives rather than extravagant lamentation or anguished stock-taking. When resistance to the Bolsheviks begins to stiffen or when the White allies fall, they apparently accept the fact that they and their supporters must pass through hell before entering paradise. They admit that change will not take place overnight, that the struggle with their opponents will be long and arduous, that the side which can preserve discipline among its troops and bolster their morale will emerge victorious. They toughen themselves for the coming campaign by reaffirming their original vows and demanding of their adherents the same fanatical devotion, which permits neither desertion nor deviation. Maryna refuses to release André from his pledge to lead her army, and both she and Luka attempt to corral those who stray from the proper ideological line: Luka insists that Ilko renounce his fanciful, idiosyncratic views and submit to the dictates of the Party, and later Maryna demands that Ilko resurrect the ideal he discarded and defend it with rigid consistency, even if it leads to a martyr's death. The most significant consequence of their fanaticism, however, is the change in their tactics. In the third act Luka and Maryna become convinced that a propaganda campaign of leaflets and fiery speeches at mass rallies will fail to sway the uncommitted and to erode the support pledged to their opponents. A new strategy, more energetic and more subtle, is conceived and carried out. The Bolsheviks secretly build up their forces from the ranks of the workers and the soldiers and prepare for a surprise raid on the town. Fearing the growing influence and power of the Reds, the nationalists ally themselves with the Whites, who will serve as a buffer against the Bolsheviks. At the same time, however, they organize their own guerrilla groups in the countryside to swoop down upon the major combatants, whose loyalties lie with Russia, after they have exhausted themselves fighting each other. Eventually even the Whites get involved in conspiratorial games, and André pretends to follow Maryna's orders while secretly deploying the partisans he commands to carry out his intentions rather than hers.

But to subdue the enemy the craftiness of subversive intrigue must be supplemented by more direct, primitive action. Violence, all are convinced, is necessary; and that is why they greet the civil war—for what other war sanctions more violence?—as a welcome opportunity to apply force continually and ruthlessly. Thus in the Ukrainian civil war no holds are barred on the field and no quarter is given the vanquished by the victors. And between skirmishes each side exerts itself to insure the swift resumption of bloody combat. The professional Bolshevik agitators encourage their troops' murderous rage against the bourgeoisie, but the nationalists and the Whites, fanning traditional class and national hatreds, are even more adept at maintaining the level of hostility at frenzied pitch: Maryna stirs up the prejudices of the local middle class and peasantry against the workers, the proletarian "riff-raff" (IV, xxiv) she so despises, and the long-smoldering resentment of all the Ukrainians against their foreign masters while the Whites, as Stupay rightly suspects in IV, viii, permit the massacre of the town's civilians not because they are Bolshevik sympathizers, but because they are Ukrainian nationals.

Though the fanaticism of Maryna, Luka, and later André (together with the attitudes and strategy it fosters) may be extolled by most revolutionary handbooks, it is not, as it appears to be, a calmly conceived, rationally planned, and intelligently developed response to the unforeseen obstacles the characters encounter. What, after all, feeds their fanaticism and stimulates its growth? Certainly not a quiet assurance of their strength, of the practicality of their goals, and of the undeniable rectitude of their ideals! If they were so confident of themselves and of the causes they serve, they would not proclaim their ideas as dogma, decree the need for eternal vigilance (recall how Luka refuses to allow anyone to sleep through the revolution in V, vii), reclaim heretics and apostates, and insist on subversion and violence as requisite tactics for the holy war. Does not their fanaticism imply that they doubt that the truths they hold are self-evident, that they suspect that human limitations, emotional instability, and intellectual uncertainty will sabotage their quest for the ideal, and that they fear that the energy liberated by this revolutionary spring, unless it is rigidly guided by ideological blinders, will sidetrack or derail their efforts to mold history? Does not their fanaticism veil a despair of their own impotence that is unobtrusive, since fanaticism is an attempt to overcome feelings of doubt, ambivalence, insecurity, and weakness? At the same time, however, it is as corrosive as it is unobtrusive, since the actions demanded by fanaticism enervate, cripple, and dehumanize them, pushing them even deeper into the quicksand they struggle against.

André's betrayal of Maryna reveals the terrible price exacted from all who flirt with subversive intrigue; the guile and deceit they employ to topple others eventually drives them to trample upon their own best instincts, interests, and virtues. Deceiving others as she herself is deceived, Maryna dupes Ilko into rescuing André from the Bolsheviks by pretending to love him and to desire his ideals:

> Forgive me, but that was not what I was going to tell you. Not that at all! Nothing about politics, but something quite different. Something more important, human and simple. All of us looked out of the windows, when we were children, and hoped that the world would be bright, and warm. As simple and intelligible as daylight, as our school primer. We cried over the body of a frozen bird. But now we are stepping over human corpses and we can't tell which of us is colder—the corpses or ourselves. Love, where have you gone from this world? Are you a dream? (*After a pause.*) Tell me, does the poet still believe in Petrarch and eternal love?
>
> * * *
>
> I will tell him about the girl who trusted the poet. She still trusts him and guards her love for him.
>
> (IV, xxiv)

Her calculated exploitation of Ilko, however, mocks everything she had once believed in, and thus she blindly denies herself the possibility of reaffirming the values of her youth—love, a fervent concern for the sanctity of life, and a passionate longing for justice.

Though Luka does not betray comrades and allies, he shares with Maryna a fierce hatred for those who oppose him, and this proves even more debilitating and destructive. Deceit only taints and perverts its practitioners, but those whose fanatical hatred feeds the flames of violence are consumed by the conflagration they fan. The first to be burned out are those who ignited the blaze, the White troops who began the civil war and were the first to slaughter civilians. Their wanton cruelty ravages them to such an extent that they can regard their handiwork, the corpse of one of their victims, with chilling callousness: "How striking and original! My opposite! His head down, my head up. When it's day for us, it's night for him and vice versa. What strange geography! Let's urinate on him!" (IV, iv). The next to share their fate and their spiritual insensateness is Georges Perotsky. He too prowls the streets—an armed killer, but a strangely mechanical figure who shoots perfunctorily at any Red crossing his path. He still responds violently, but it seems to him that his gun fires by itself, for he pulls the trigger without feeling any human emotion, neither pleasure nor pain, neither joy nor horror: "Today I killed one of them. You know how it happened? He ran from behind a corner straight into me. My gun fired and he fell. Have you got some candy? Just a little? By the way the sign blew off the sweetshop. The wind tore it off. Later the wind dropped. Guns were firing" (IV, xxx). Luka and Maryna, it is true, do not sink to the subhuman level of these men: they are not completely destroyed by the fire of violence, but the smoke produced by the morally rotten fuel they supply envelops them and slowly begins to suffocate them, to choke their emotions and their reason, to stifle their humanity. Quite unexpectedly Luka insists that all men are puppets or machines subservient to external commands or demands—orders from the Party? instinctual impulses?—which they obey without judgment and without feeling. In his new world view even love is mechanized, for "Love is not an escape and a dream, as it was with Ilko, but a function. Yes, a function! That reminds me, I have a meeting where I am to talk about the new functions of my sub-sections" (V, i). And it has already been pointed out that Maryna loses her sanity as she responds to the oracle of her diseased imagination and demands from the Ukrainians more ferocious resistance to the enemy.

The dehumanization of Luka and Maryna begins, oddly enough, at the moment when he has attained power and she is on the verge of assuming power through a counterrevolutionary coup, at the moment when their tactics have proved successful or will soon prove so. But their success is not prized: rather than consolidating or planning to consolidate their gains (restoring order, resting their troops, rewarding the faithful, indoctrinating those who have resisted, etc.), both levy greater demands upon themselves and their followers. The first taste of power, even the first whiff of it, is so heady that they become addicts whose craving can never be satisfied. Consequently, they refuse to relax or relinquish the tactics that have been so effective and instead advocate their retention and amplification. When Zinka asks Luka for work, he replies that the Bolsheviks cannot offer her the meaningful labor she hopes will dignify and justify her existence since at this stage of the revolution the party must concentrate on pursuing and annihilating its opponents: "There'll be plenty of work. Not during the first stage of the revolution when fighting and destruction are going on. But after that there'll be work" (V, i). A few scenes later Maryna echoes these strange thoughts, stating that the present task of the nationalists is not to win independence for Ukraine, but to harass all their opponents, to disrupt by means of sustained guerrilla warfare all attempts to end the civil war and create order out of chaos:

> No matter how strong the wind from the north it won't blow out the fire. No, it will intensify it. Blow until the sparks fly!... Omphalos! Light your pipes so that the smoke spreads across the steppe and into the heavens. Smoke until the sky is dense with it, until God sends you an angel who, as in a folktale, will ask you: "What do you want, you Cossacks, who have smoked so much?" We want our own state under this flag. . . .
>
> (V, iii)

Whereas Luka and Maryna had formerly resolved to subdue their foes swiftly and had consciously chosen violence as a primitive but expedient means to force on others certain specific goals, the socio-political transformation of Ukraine or its liberation from foreign domination, they now demand the complete destruction of the enemy or his continual harassment and project into the misty future the attainment of those goals they had so passionately desired. What they now advocate and apply is violence drained of all positive content and moral purpose, violence for the sake of violence, violence to slake their blood lust.

Even the reality of defeat cannot temper the addictive obsession with violence. All experience major setbacks, since no faction can hold the town for any significant length of time. The vanquished retreat, regroup, and return to the attack. The only achievement of the strategy of the combatants is the littering of the ground with corpses. Many are killed, many sacrifice themselves, but all fall in vain, with the ends they support far from realization. Yet in the face of constant failure they neither review nor change their tactics but are sucked deeper into the morass of subversion and force that has dehumanized them and blasted their hopes: driven underground and threatened by exposure, Maryna continues to plan her campaign of terror while Luka, the temporary victor at the end of the play, prepares for the sitting of the revolutionary tribunal whose proceedings will be as deliberate and just as the White court it displaces.

The responsibility for the increase in violence does not, however, lie solely with Luka, Maryna, and André, the leaders of the contending factions. It must also be borne by the ordinary citizens of the town, people like Ovram and Zinka who come to accept violence as the central fact of life and fail to oppose its cancerous growth. Maimed by the past, Ovram and Zinka are reborn in this revolutionary spring and desire a new life for themselves—a quiet, normal, decent life. To the best of their abilities they support the Bolsheviks to achieve this goal, only to be mocked cruelly by the civil war that claims their dreams and their lives. The continuation of the old violence that had already cost Ovram his legs and Zinka her self-respect shatters whatever hope they had for a different life, and they submit fatalistically to the bestiality and brutality they see around them. Ovram, crushed by the scattering of the Bolsheviks when attacked by André's troops, desperately urges his fleeing comrades to make a suicidal stand rather than retreat in cowardly fashion to fight and die another day, "You can't run away from death. Stand still!" (V, ix). The weird bravado of this shout is heard again when he taunts his captors and judges and when he faces execution, perversely fortified by the knowledge that his death will be viciously avenged. In the same courtroom Zinka, who had attempted to resist the senseless violence of the civil war by handing Georges over to the Bolsheviks after he refused to stop firing his gun, confesses her crime to the court thirsting for the blood of Georges's betrayer. Her confession, unlike Ovram's, is not a reckless and defiant political gesture; it is an act of capitulation of a woman tormented and exhausted by the violence swirling about her, by the Bolsheviks' proclamation of total warfare, and by the vengeful acts of their foes. In the end both Ovram and Zinka bow their heads to violence, he jauntily perpetuating it and she wearily seeking release from it.

With the suicidal submission of both major and minor characters to the growing violence of the revolution, the sobering truth of Ilko's opening comment, marking the spring of 1917 as an apocalyptic spring, becomes readily apparent. At first the energy of this spring had freed the populace of the town from slavery, from a state of demeaning bondage to the old, routine patterns of thought and action. Spiritually and physically they were exhilarated, spurred to dream of a higher, more noble life for themselves and for others and to act for the realization of these dreams. They set to work vigorously, even violently; but their forceful, intense activity was directed at counteracting the destructive violence of this revolutionary spring, at harnessing the rampant energy of the spring torrents to build the world they envisioned. These heroic efforts, however, were short-lived for, as they were denied an outlet for the expression of their ideals, their bodies and minds bent under the pressure of the energy that inundated them. Colliding with a reality that was not malleable they reacted to the painful recognition of their impotence by releasing and diverting some of this pent-up energy, hoping to use it to impose a more limited order, an ideologically appropriate form, on reality. When this goal eluded them, their loathing for everything that thwarted them (their own weakness as well as the intractability of reality) grew so intense that it crumbled all the controls and restraints they had maintained on the energy of this spring. As their faith in themselves and others eroded and as their heroic vision of the individual's value and dignity collapsed, violence, which had been considered a calculated risk and a temporary measure, became a desperate need. It became a facile means of asserting themselves and relieving the anxiety produced by constant failure and frustration; it obliterated everyone, themselves included, and everything that testified to their inadequacy and insubstantiality. So hypnotized were they by the power that violence conferred that they sacrificed to it their emotions, their reason, and their dreams. Without any real hope of alleviating their own fortunes and without any desire to end the civil war, they either surrendered to the tide of barbarism they had unleashed or decided to ride its crest, preferring destruction to accommodation with stasis, inertia, or lack of change, and choosing annihilation over an impoverished existence in a cold, stagnant, and hated world.

The rhythm of *Sonata Pathetique* clearly depicts this entire process, showing how the energy presses against the barriers constructed against it and how, when freed from human control, it inundates the land, swirling about at its own dynamic pace and sucking everything in its path into its destructive

27

vortex. The inevitable end to this process, as Stupay perceives moments before his death, is total catastrophe:

> Well, I've risen. But I don't know which side I should join. (*He thinks and hesitates.*) Neither this side nor that. (*The bullets whiz by.*) Wait. There are Ukrainians on both sides. What are you doing? Let me think! They're firing at each other, glad that they have ammunition. . . . (*A flower, cut by a bullet, falls to the ground. Stupay picks it up.*) So they'll destroy all the flowers, will kill mother earth, the wheat, the sunflowers—what are you doing?
>
> (V, ix)

Ukraine and all living in it will be devastated, for no one can possibly surface from the whirlpool of revolutionary conflict. Not even the hero Ilko Yuha, who had so valiantly struggled against the seductive allure of violence, can escape being caught in the undertow. And the implications of Ilko's fall cast the final, sombre hue upon Kulish's bleak vision of revolution in the modern world.

In the last act of *Sonata Pathetique* the specific issues of the play are brilliantly summarized and darkly resolved as Ilko, a shepherd's son and an intellectual, a poet and a fighter, a narrator and an actor—in short, a Ukrainian everyman—faces his third and last crisis in which he must resolve a thoroughly conventional dramatic conflict: he wants to decide between love and duty or, extended to its more particular manifestations in this play, between the rights of the individual and the rights of society, between nationalism and Bolshevism. His problem here is similar to the problems he had faced previously and involves the same choice between alternative values and the modes of action issuing from them. Earlier he had taken a definite stand, committing himself to the Petrarchan ideal of love in the first act and then devoting himself to the cause of social revolution in the fourth act. But he had never insisted dogmatically that love and duty were mutually incompatible. His dream was broader than the dreams of others, his allegiances less inflexible than theirs: thus, the lover could be persuaded by Luka to become a part-time political activist, and the Bolshevik revolutionary was easily swayed by Maryna to save André in the name of love. Though his faith in his ability to harmonize the conflicting demands of self and society faltered occasionally, Ilko never questioned the validity of his desire to yoke these extremes. Only after the execution of Ovram and Zinka does he realize how unenlightened and destructive his attempt at synthesis had proved:

I was sent by Hamar, but she saw me on the stairs and asked me to save André Perotsky. I saved him. She was my dream and for two years I raced after that vision through the steppes, although she lived a few yards away from me. Then she asked me to save the man who was our enemy. How could I not show kindness and love? I was detached from the masses, lost somewhere in the attic between heaven and earth. My thoughts were the cobweb of a dreamer, who thought he could reconcile heaven and earth. I was a dreamer who wanted to find a bridge between the ideal and the mob, between the nation and its future. The result is familiar: the ruin and death of comrades, a dead interval in the revolutionary struggle. I am the author of that interval, Luka!

(VII, iv)

Aware that he had been duped into freeing André, Ilko nevertheless experiences such enormous guilt for the death of his friends (note that he blames himself for the 'dead interval') that he feels he must finally separate and choose between his two ideals, the ideal of love (which Maryna intimately binds to the cause of Ukrainian nationalism) and the ideal of duty (which Luka ties to the cause of Bolshevism). Because of his utopian longing for a "revolution with a human face," Ilko is determined to select that ideology which fully reflects his inordinate faith in man and in the potentiality of human nature, an ideology which can unite all in harmonious accord, elevate them morally, and upon this high and solid foundation inspire them to construct for themselves an ideal social system.

That Ilko rejects nationalism is in no way surprising or unexpected, since the play has already examined rigorously two major strands of nationalism, represented by Stupay and Maryna, and has bared their critical flaws and weaknesses. Stupay is a romantic nationalist, a cultural nationalist concerned with the problem of national identity:

The Russians stole Hlynka from us and say that he is their Glinka. He's not Glinka but Hlynka. A Ukrainian surname—he must be Ukrainian. But from now on, Maryna, we won't give up any Ukrainians. I plan to go out into the streets at once, to churches, wherever there are people and demonstrate in favor of a free Ukraine. Now every Ukrainian, before he goes to sleep, must think about Ukraine and must get up in the morning with his country as his chief concern. First, let's rebuild it and then we'll support internationalism. That's the way to do it, not the way you write about it, comrade Bolsheviks. How can internationalism exist without Ukraine, without the *bandura*?

(I, ix)

Insistent about the rejection of everything Russian, Stupay wants his countrymen to speak their own language, to appreciate the achievements of Ukrainian artists, and to revere the primitive democracy established in the Sich by the Zaporozhian Cossacks. Glorifying the moral grandeur of his country's culture, he strives to awaken national self-consciousness and national pride in the hope that the Ukrainians, like their ancestors, will band together, purge the land of the foreign masters, and then build an autonomous, democratic state that will serve as a vibrant model for other countries to emulate. Maryna's nationalism, on the other hand, is more up to date, political, and militant. She too idealizes the past but, unlike her father, who admires the Cossacks as defenders of the integrity of Ukraine and protectors of its borders, she recalls lovingly the glorious military triumphs of old and the heroic hetmen who conquered the Poles and the Russians. She reminds others of the vigor and might of the old Cossack state rather than its cultural achievements, and she campaigns actively for a strong, independent Ukraine, an armed Ukraine that will stand not as a superior moral example, but as an aggressive, dynamic rival in competition with other major nations for land, markets, and power.

The grand illusions of father and daughter are easily punctured. Stupay's position collapses first. Indeed, it does not even get a fair hearing from the people he hopes to enlist in his cause because his nationalism fails to offer them what they need. The immediate desires of the masses are personal rather than nationalistic, prosaic rather than poetic, materialistic rather than idealistic, and so they shout down his sentimental glorification of Zaporozhian Cossack life and his reverence for such intangible abstractions as language, art, and ideal political institutions:

> Stupay: It's time to be free! Let's ride our horses and race across the steppes with the eagles and the winds. . . .

> * * *

> Ovram: You may be all right, but what are you going to do about us?
> Stupay: About whom?
> Ovram: About me—a legless Ukrainian proletarian (*pointing to the bootblacks*) and about them?
> Zinka: (*comes out of the crowd, a little tipsy*): And what about me? Back under the saddle or on the mattress?

> (III, iv)

Ovram and the other men want bread and work, not high-sounding principles and romantic visions. Zinka the prostitute wants what was denied women in Cossack society—equality of status and opportunity. For them to accept Stupay's ideal means continued exploitation and not liberation.

Stupay's nationalism is undermined by the lack of mass support; Maryna's by her rejection of this support. She cannot see any reason to win over people whom she despises for their obstinate concern with personal survival. Instead of addressing the rabble she turns toward the restless, patriotic youth of the nation's higher classes, for whom she revives those features of the national past that will inspire them to assert themselves, to flex their muscles, and to wrest from others fame, glory, and power. Hence her demand for the restoration of Cossack militarism and of the institutions, mores, and values generated by past eras of political turmoil and war rather than by previous periods of stability and peace. Once again Ukraine must be ruled by a hetman, a man of action to lead the nation against its traditional enemies, a general to assemble and train an efficient and ruthless war machine, and a dictator to purge the country of all who cannot be persuaded to join the army—the dreamers, intellectuals, nonconformists—or who are unfit to join the ranks of this elite corps of warriors—the weak, the proletarian "riff raff," the politically suspect. The purification of Ukraine through the suppression of protest and the repression of minority groups may facilitate Maryna's desire to breed a hardy and superior Cossack stock powerful enough to conquer the world, but more disastrous long-range effects are more probable. The forced regimentation of the country will in all likelihood destroy both the strong and the weak, the oppressors and the oppressed. Those selected to dominate the new society, given ideological justification for their inherent prejudices against all who challenge the supremacy of their class, way of life, and values, will be unable to control and restrain themselves when offered a chance to express their vindictiveness and hate, and the purge they conduct will soon turn into a blood bath. If not massacred, those rejected as inferior will either resist savagely their persecution or will submit coldly and numbly to enslavement, responding apathetically to the will of their masters. In any event, the nation as a whole will be fatally divided or seriously weakened. Maryna's ultimate goal, therefore, is undermined by her rejection of everything her father values. Though she correctly criticizes his indiscriminate adulation of Ukrainian culture, ridiculing the "calico pants" and other silly aspects of the national mythology that he wants to revive, she fails to appreciate that Ukraine can re-establish itself as a major world state only with the united support of all its people. And this national unity, the solidarity of rich and poor, talented and mediocre, strong and weak, intellectual and Cossack, worker and peasant, can be forged only if all respect their common heritage and strive to preserve their own language, their indigenous traditions, and their distinctive culture.

Though Ilko's acceptance of Bolshevism seems as inevitable as his rejection of nationalism, this affirmation is very disturbing not because it leads him to turn Maryna over to her enemies—after all, Ilko does not make this decision without struggle and then admits honestly his unwitting collaboration in her conspiracy—but because the absolute commitment to Bolshevism relieves him of the burden of guilt for his act of betrayal, blinds him to the dangerous consequences of his own confession, and permits him to view the future with groundless optimism. Moreover, his final decision to support Luka, while it does give him the strength necessary to resist Maryna's attempts to break his resolve, does not enable him to counter her criticism of his final stance. Her trenchant queries and comments he can rebut but not confute. Her weakest objection— that he is betraying his country and agreeing to continued Russian control of Ukraine—cannot be swept aside lightly by questioning the value of patriotism. Somehow Ilko will prolong the "Russian night," the end of which was promised at the opening of the play. The Ukrainian Bolsheviks imitate their Russian models even in the lip service they pay to the principle of internationalism, a slogan that the partisan soldiers chant without understanding its meaning and a piety that the leaders mouth to smother the nationalistic aspirations of the people they hope to rule. Maryna's main question, however, is whether Ilko's ultimate goal, the creation of a political structure solid enough to safeguard the rights of all its members and yet spacious enough to guarantee the unfettered development of each and every individual and group, can be attained by the Bolsheviks. Their aim is lower than Ilko's and, she maintains, her own. Their main concerns are justice rather than freedom, equality of opportunity rather than the encouragement of personal initiative, the leveling of society to its lowest common denominator rather than its elevation through the achievements of its most vital, exceptional, and creative individuals:

> She: I would play for you but they've separated me from my piano. What good is it to them? Who on their side can play? Tell me, who will play the piano?
>
> I: Don't worry, they'll play.
>
> She: Will they play the *Pathetique*?
>
> I: First of all.

To this objection Ilko responds with a fervent declaration of his faith in the people, in their creativity and their desire to transform Beethoven's sonata into a symphony. At the very end of the play he identifies the potential of the masses with the energy of the cosmos pulsating in the night, already playing the symphony about which he dreams, and calling upon all sensitive and sympathetic listeners, among whom Ilko erroneously lists Luka, to follow its example. But he neglects to ask himself how all this energy will be focused upon this proper and worthy end. Who will teach the masses to respect their creativity? Who will help them to learn Beethoven's music and urge them to orchestrate it? Where are all the creative people, the artists, lovers, and dreamers, who could guide and inspire the unfortunate, the underprivileged, and the handicapped to display properly the power that is within them? Only a handful of people with talent, vision, and faith will survive the civil war, and of the survivors none will be called upon to help in the restructuring of society, since the Bolsheviks disdain intellectuals and dreamers as much as the nationalists do. And Ilko Yuha, the last dreamer in the world of the play, must soon appear before the revolutionary tribunal, which will certainly not be satisfied with Luka's testimony on behalf of his friend; the tribunal will demand of the defendant a full recantation of past errors, a renunciation of his dream, and a promise of total subservience to the directives of the Party.

When the final curtain drops, Ilko is alone on stage, oblivious to his imminent downfall. This terrible end, however, must not be attributed to the fact that he chose Luka over Maryna, for his situation would not be altered if he had decided to join Maryna. The bitter irony of his final dilemma is that it matters little whether he decides to help the Bolsheviks extinguish the flame of nationalism or to keep Maryna's candle lit. If he shared with her a feverish, disordered life, it would not be in the rarefied atmosphere of his attic hermitage (perhaps an allusion to exile as a safe, distant haven where, Maryna realizes, the idea of national liberation would soon die out), but in the dark, damp underground recently vacated by the Bolsheviks.

Neither alternative can hasten the end of the fratricidal war destroying Ukraine and its people, and neither alternative can possibly satisfy Ilko's utopian yearnings. His fall, therefore, is due not to a wrong choice but to his decision to choose between drastically restricted and restrictive options. By limiting himself to this traditional and conventional set of alternatives he involves himself in the same petty drama of commitment that his contemporaries have already experienced, and he fails to grasp the real opportunity presented him by revolution to enact a much greater and more significant drama. Ilko's failure, which is essentially that of all the major figures of the play, is a failure of imagination, a fatal hesitancy to continue his utopian quest, to invent new affirmations, to conceive of new truths, to create new myths, and thereby to transform radically the structure and the content of reality.

None of the characters in *Sonata Pathetique* are able to "seize the day." Early in the play Ilko and Luka argue about the different paths they have chosen, justifying their positions on the basis of historical precedent:

> I: Guess, what's the way the world has inevitably followed for thousands of years?
> Luka (*having understood that I am hopelessly in love, with grim determination*): The way of revolution!
> I: The way of love! Guess, Luka, without what would the world have long ago wandered like a eunuch across the desert of life?
> Luka: Without the way of revolution, . . .

(II, i)

Each proudly points to the past just as Stupay and Maryna turn backwards to bolster their different types of nationalism. This sanctification of the past blinds them to present reality and its fertile shapelessness and compels them to assume certain patterns of emotion, thought, and action that have been played out and proven inadequate for hundreds and thousands of years. The point that Kulish emphasizes is that nationalism and Bolshevism are not new, revolutionary innovations created in response to the realities of modern life but dusty relics of old beliefs that allow the dead hand of the past to vitiate the present and to deform the future. No matter how grand and heroic the imaginative flights of the characters, their idealism carries within itself from the very moment of its resurgence the seeds of its own destruction. It is built of old, rotten timbers—old commitments, fossilized ideas, traditional ends that have been used and reused for so long that, exhausted by age and use, they cannot manage to withstand and control the explosive pressures of modern revolution, the anarchic compulsions of modern life, and the destructive impulses of modern man. Only one voice in the play, a prophetic voice from the past, fully understands the tragic bondage that crippled the Ukrainians in former times and continues to sap their strength in the present. The voice is that of Shevchenko, who cried out in his testament, "Bury me and then rise up." But the living remain deaf to this authentic revolutionary imperative calling for the complete rejection of archaic values and obsolete models of thought and behavior, and their replacement with fresh dreams and original modes of perception and action uncontaminated by the past.

This general discussion of *Sonata Pathetique* has necessarily slighted much of value and importance in the drama: the presence of a narrator; the language of the play, especially the brilliant use of images and motifs from folk literature; the impressive aural effects, which build on Beethoven's music, military marches, and lullabies to heighten the various moods of the acts; the emotional impact of even the most epigrammatic scenes, such as the poignant moment when Nastia offers Luka her own boots rather than those of her legless husband or the funny but pathetic quarrel between Stupay and old Perotsky about basic principles at the very moment when the revolution is shattering the world in which these principles were meaningful; and other features of craft and content. Too much stress, perhaps, has been placed on the revolutionary experience that the play embodies, but it is this aspect of the work that reveals the relevance and power of Kulish's vision. Excited by the outbreak of revolution and horrified by its development, Kulish depicts clearly the cannibalistic process by which the revolution consumes the creatures it spawns. And yet, *Sonata Pathetique* is not a reactionary tract repudiating revolution, which is, after all, presented as the central experience of man in the modern world. Rather, the play discloses the conservative impulses and forces in its characters. These impulses keep them from responding openly to the opportunity revolution provides to reject the past, to move beyond previous failures and accomplishments, and to liberate themselves from all the old aesthetic, social, political, religious, and philosophical assumptions—no matter how base or noble, empty or productive, they were—so that new and different conceptions of man and society, uninvestigated possibilities of life, can be voiced and explored.

From this perspective the revolution proves degrading and destructive rather than elevating and creative, because revolutionary idealism either is swamped by a sentimentalism that refuses to jettison the ballast of the past or is subverted by a fanaticism that, doubting man's heroic stature and creativity, cannot acknowledge that "man's reach should exceed his grasp." The revolutionary dream to create a new man and a new environment for him is, therefore, fated to remain unfulfilled, since both the ideals and the actions of the dreamers fail to match the radical thrust and scope of their aspirations. All too rapidly the desire to cross the frontiers of the actual and the possible in order to transform reality vanishes. It is replaced by the urge to reform the world, to renovate and restore the old order rather than rebuild it, or by the insane impulse to demolish the old, condemned system without any imaginative conception of the structure to be built on the rubble. Whatever the ultimate response to the revolution, the possibility of significant change is lost, and the characters of Kulish's world are doomed to wander in the perpetual darkness of the world they want to destroy, clawing at one another in hell's most vicious circle and condemning themselves to unrelieved, unredeemed pain and suffering.

— *Ralph Lindheim*

Sonata Pathetique was written in 1930. Kulish wanted to see it performed in Ukraine but was unable to obtain permission to produce it. He thereupon sent the play to Moscow, where it was translated into Russian and staged, with great success, by the famous producer Tairov in the Kamerny Theater on December 20, 1931. The play was produced in Leningrad simultaneously. However, after a very successful run in Moscow, the play was discontinued at the end of March following an attack which appeared in *Pravda* condemning the play as nationalist. Nothing more was heard of the play and a few years later the author was arrested and deported. Mykola Kulish died in a concentration camp in 1937. His death brought to an end an era of truly exceptional achievement in Ukrainian drama and theater. Kulish found an ideal collaborator in Les Kurbas (1885-1942), the director of the *Berezil** theater from 1922 to 1933. Departing sharply from the traditional ethnographic theater, *Berezil* succeeded in creating a truly modern, strongly expressionist, Ukrainian theater. Apart from many foreign plays and new adaptations of old Ukrainian plays, *Berezil* successfully staged three other plays by Kulish: *Myna Mazailo*, *The People's Malakhii*, and *Maklena Grasa*. In 1933 the theater was disbanded after charges of nationalism and formalism were voiced against it in the press. Kurbas shared Kulish's tragic fate.

Sonata Pathetique was first published in 1943 in Cracow, under the German occupation. The text was shortened a little to accommodate the German censorship. The same text was reprinted in the collected works of Kulish published in New York in 1955. In Ukraine, Kulish was partially rehabilitated in

---

*For a study of the *Berezil* by one of the original members see: Y. Hirniak, "Birth and Death of the Modern Ukrainian Theater," in M. Bradshaw (ed.), *Soviet Theaters: 1917-1941* (New York, 1954).

the late 1950's and the play was published in 1968 and 1969. It was also staged for the first time in Ukraine in Odessa, in 1958, and later in Kiev in 1966. According to reliable reports, both productions were almost complete distortions of the original play.

The text of the play that appeared in 1968 differs considerably from the 1943-1955 text. In this translation it has been decided to follow the recent Soviet text rather than the obviously truncated 1943-1955 version. Yet certain passages which appear in the earlier, incomplete version have been included. The most important of these is the scene of Stupay's death, which the later Soviet version omits. There is no doubt that just as the 1943 version excluded pro-Soviet passages to please the German censorship, so the 1968 version excluded anti-Soviet passages. It is, of course, impossible today to restore the original version of the play,* and one should not rule out the possibility that, under the pressure of Soviet censorship, Kulish himself revised the first version. What is offered here is the fullest available text, with the risk that the overall balance may be in favor of the late Soviet version. This is especially so in the last act of the play, which was badly cut in the earlier version. It is translated here from the 1968 text and it may well distort the original ending of the play. Yet on balance it was decided to include this fuller, although possibly doctored, act. A special victim of the present ending of the play is the heroine, Maryna, who no longer behaves as heroically as she did in the earlier, shorter version. In other variants Maryna is killed by Ilko; here she cringes and vacillates to the end. The downgrading of Maryna might have been the price Kulish was willing to pay to see his play performed. The final scene of the last act ends with a communist victory. Yet this victory is hollow, for, as Professor Lindheim points out in his introduction, the revolution has indeed destroyed all its children, including the communists. The central meaning of the play is enhanced by the hero's delusion that at last he is hearing a "symphony pathetique." In fact, as in Beethoven's sonata, the finale is not as happy as it sounds.

—George S. N. Luckyj

---

*In a remarkably objective recent study of Kulish (Kiev, 1970) N. Kuziakina mentions that Kulish was continually changing his play and as a result several variants exist, some of them still unpublished.

Sonata Pathetique

CAST OF CHARACTERS

I (Ilko Yuha) . . . . a poet
She (Maryna Stupay-Stupanenko) . . . . a student of music
Ivan Stupay-Stupanenko . . . . Maryna's father
Perotsky . . . . a Russian general
André, Georges . . . . his sons
Anette . . . . Perotsky's housekeeper
Zinka . . . . a prostitute
Ovram . . . . a worker
Nastia . . . . his wife
Luka . . . . a communist
Hamar . . . . a Bolshevik agitator
Comrade Fate, also called sailor
Workers, sailors, partisans, citizens, people in the street

ACT ONE

1

Imagine, my friends, he started to say: 1) a street in an old, provincial city, 2) a three-story building with a sign "the residence of Major-General Perotsky," 3) a revolutionary spring, 4) Easter night. The beginning of action: I am writing. A semi-attic in the building. A square window with a starry sky for a curtain. A gas lamp is burning. In the corner there shines a coiled brass helicon.

2

Next to me, behind a wooden partition lives an unemployed milliner Zinka. She is combing her hair. There are visitors at her door.

First Visitor (*reading a sign written in chalk on the door*): "Because it is Easter I do not receive guests." (*A pause; with annoyance*) Ha! That's clever!

Second Visitor (*jealously, in a bass voice*): Why have you stopped?

First Visitor: Where shall we go now?

Second Visitor: At Easter each hostess has her door open.

First Visitor: So I'll go to your hostess. All right?

3

Zinka is laughing. The visitors, annoyed, are leaving. I am writing. Underneath in the general's apartment the clock strikes, as if from a distant age, evenly, nostalgically, elegiacally. Further below, on the first floor—she lives. I can almost see it: the open window and the windblown curtain like a sail. A corner of a well-lit room is seen with a piano, Shevchenko's bust and flowers. She is practising Beethoven's Sonata Pathetique. She plays the first movement, the deep and mighty grave, full of starry pathos. (At that time I knew neither the composer nor the work.)

4

Zinka knocks on my door.

May I come in? Tell me, neighbor, when a girl is visited by many men and she wants to run away from them, what does it mean?

I: I don't know.

Zinka: And why they all want to break the fast and she wants to go on fasting, do you know what that means?

I: I can't say.

Zinka: Don't you really know? And can't you guess? What are you? It is so simple. It means that there came . . .love, do you think? It is Easter night! That's all. And immediately you begin to think.

(I am shaking my head.)

Zinka: Ha-ha! Going to church, for example. But you are thinking of something else. *(She winks.)* Don't worry. You won't break Lent because of me.

I: I am not worried. You see, I don't have the time. I am writing a letter.

Zinka: You are writing. Excuse me. Go on writing. I'd like to write a letter too. I would write: In the twenty-third year of my life a red day in the calendar and a black one in my heart. People used to say that when freedom came it would be like your own mother to you. They said that a girl would have a good time, that the world would be full of sunshine and flowers. Now freedom has come. And here I am writing: darling . . . and no one answers. . . . Good night. By the way, you couldn't lend me some money— seven rubles? They're asking for my rent. I'll pay you back. I'll get the money for my room (*she winks*) and I'll pay you back. Don't have any? Go on writing.

5

Stone steps leading from the first floor down into the dark basement. Two people are sorting out illegal literature. To one side, a woman is ironing. Water keeps dripping from time to time, resonantly and persistently, from the ceiling into a bucket.

Elderly Man (*putting aside leaflets*): This goes to the Vadony factory. Now for the dock workshops—the brochures "When the war ends"—one, two, three, four, five. . . . (*A drop falls; he turns and looks at the ceiling, the bucket, and resumes counting.*) Seven, eight, nine, ten. (*Another drop falls; he frowns.*) Does your ceiling always drip?

Woman: This is the third year. It started when my husband, Ovram, joined up. Since then I have waited and counted the drops. It takes seven drops to wash a shirt and ten to iron it. Do you know how many drops fall during a day? Four hundred and thirty times ten. How many is that?

Elderly Man: 43,000.

Woman: I wait and I count. My head is like a sieve. My whole life is like a sieve—the drops have made holes in it. I remember I began counting them the first Sunday after Easter. (*Counting the drops*) One, two. When I saw him off I said: but you are a coppersmith, Ovram. You have grown hard of hearing in the factory, but they have drafted you. And he said to me . . . three . . . that's why they are drafting us because we are deaf and blind. And he went. It was misty, and you couldn't see the gate. I called after him: Ovram, but he didn't turn around . . . Four. . . . When can

44

I expect him back? He didn't turn round. At the factory he stopped. I ran and caught up with him. Just then. . . . Five. . . . It was six o'clock and the siren went. He never used to cry, but I saw him listening to that siren and crying. . . . Six. . . . Tell me, what is the biggest number?

Elderly Man: A quadrillion.

Woman: Quadrillion. If someone told me that when the quadrillionth drop fell the war would end and my Ovram would come back, I would count every drop, not miss one. (*Passionately, with tears in her eyes*) I would string those drops like beads. (*Standing, as if in prayer, she counts the drops.*) Seven. . .eight. . .nine. . . .

Young Man: Sister, you again . . .

Woman: Eight, nine, ten.

Young Man (*to the elderly one*): What can you do?

Elderly Man (*sternly*): What? Distribute literature! Organize! Agitate! We must fire the whole world with our slogans. . . .

Young Man: I have a friend here. Shall I call him?

Elderly Man: Who is he?

Young Man: A student.

Elderly Man (*making a wry face*): Hm!

Young Man: Not a regular student. He's studying at home through the university extension. His father is a shepherd. The boy is a little bit of a dreamer, but he's reliable—one of us.

Elderly Man: Seven! Call him!

6

My best friend and comrade comes to me.

Luka: Hello, Ilko, what are you doing?

I (*with some pathos*): I am writing her a letter.

Luka: The one hundred and thirtieth?

I: Don't laugh, Luka.

Luka: Are you going to tear it up soon?

I: Don't you dare. You don't know the mood I'm in. (*Below I hear the chords.*) I feel as tall and bright as the sky. First (*pointing to the helicon*) do you see this? It is called a helicon. When you blow a *forte* on it you can blow out a lamp. But I shall learn to play it well enough to blow out the stars in the sky.

Luka (*ironically*): What for?

I: Just to keep myself busy.

Luka: You'll be busy, but will you have a job?

I: A job too. This helicon is from a band which plays in summer on the boulevards, in the fall at weddings and in the winter at funerals, a very humane band. There are heliconists who manage to squeeze out of this boa a sound like a silver bell. Just like this: boom, boom. (*Just then the clock strikes below.*) And I'll learn how! I must! But the most important thing is: I'm writing her a letter. (*From underneath I notice how, after the* grave, *there rolls the first wave of the brilliant* allegro molto e con brio.) Listen! (*I read and improvise.*) Perhaps I'll tear this one up, but I write and shall go on writing because I believe in Petrarch and eternal love. In love eternal. Besides, golden figures cast black shadows in history, but from the monastic figure of Petrarch there falls a bright, golden reflection— that of eternal love. I believe and I write. You are playing something new today, I don't know what it is, but this music is certainly about a young man who is racing on horseback through the steppes in search of the land of eternal love. A solitary girl stands at a blue window. Her left brow is raised a little, as if her blue eyes are smiling. Tell me, winds or stars, will the girl go out to meet him, will she open the doors, the beautiful gates to the land of eternal love? (*Half-crying and half-laughing*) Guess, Luka. . . .

Luka: The gates are there to be opened.

I: No, not that. Guess, will I send this letter or not?

Luka: Whatever you did with the hundred and thirty earlier ones.

I (*solemnly and categorically*): I'll do it today. I'll take it myself.

Luka: Today we have to give out the literature, and you must help us. Let's go!

I: We'll take it tomorrow.

Luka: You want to postpone the cause of social revolution till tomorrow?

I: Not really. But remember Luka: a bloody flag of struggle is fluttering over the world. What for? So that tomorrow the banner of free labor may fly over us. But this will happen only when the flags of eternal love rise over the whole world. . . .

Luka: To hell with your eternal love! Today at the trade union meeting a comrade from Petrograd told us that we must do everything to let the train of the revolution go full speed to socialism. And you want to stop it at the station . . . (*mockingly*) "Eternal Love."

I (*annoyed and offended, after he turns to go*): Only when the man who beats his wife today becomes a Petrarch, will the universal social spring come. And you say: to hell with it. You've misunderstood the whole problem.

7

I almost follow Luka. I am carrying a letter. At any other time I would have torn it up, as I did a hundred and thirty times before. But now I am forced to deliver it. And so I am carrying it down the steps leading to where she lives. But how shall I deliver it? I walk further down. I can see that from the basement an elderly worker carrying bundles of literature is emerging. He is followed by Luka. Nastia gives him a piece of Easter cake and some Easter eggs. She whispers:

Take it. You can eat it on the way.

Luka: What's that? (*To the elderly man, pointing to the Easter eggs*) Shall we take it, comrade Hamar? It's religious!

Elderly Man: Take it. We'll eat it all the same!

In order not to meet Luka I go back upstairs. Through Perotsky's door I can hear the clock striking. After that the sound of the electric doorbell. Perotsky's voice to his housekeeper:

A telegram from André from the front: "Obtained leave. Arriving on the first at six." He's going to be here in half an hour. Anette, get the bath and bedclothes ready! And please tell me how much you spent today. Don't be offended, Anette. I trust you and will go on trusting you, but at this time of revolution it is necessary to keep strict accounts. Thank you, Anette. (*Reading*) Three locks for doors: 11 rubles 73 kopeks. But for smashing the Russian crown, Anette, you should charge the revolutionaries. As well as for time lost through a strike of workers at my mill. Whom shall we charge for bromide, us or them? Don't dare buy it. Where there is the smell of bromide there will soon be the smell of corpses. Don't you dare! Receipts: rent from Stupay-Stupanenko—10 rubles and 15 kopeks. That's all? What about the rent for the mezzanine? And for the basement? Evict them. I'm not afraid of their revolution! The one thing I am afraid of is that the foundation on which Russia rests, its unity and indivisibility, should be preserved. It will not be destroyed by Stupay-Stupanenkos. Russia will survive and weather all revolutions. ·Russia! The Russian land! Rus'! Where is this beautiful music coming from? Anette, my dear, get me my uniform from the closet. I shall go to church. Anette, do you remember the Easter Monday of 1913, the birch tree outside the window and the dawn? Russia was all fragrant then—and now, Anette! Attention! I'm trying to regiment my thoughts . . . such chaos! Anette, keep expenditures down! In a ceremonial march, column, left march!

It is quiet. He must have gone because I hear another voice. It is Perotsky's son—Georges:

Well, my dear Anette?

Anette: Georges, your papa has told me to keep expenditures down.

Georges: I'll give it back to you. I give you the word of a future officer. I'll return it.

Anette: Georges, you must understand, there is no money.

Georges: My word of honor, I'll give it back. You should know that in a month or two our class of cadets will become officer-cadets. I'll go to war! Against the Bolsheviks! I'll click my heels, look into the mirror and see (*in a fantasy*) a young officer with shining epaulettes, black mustache. . . .

Anette: You are my dreaming boy!

Georges: A boy? (*On purpose tries to be brutal but sounds naive.*) A young officer with five condoms in his pocket—what will you say to that, my beauty queen?

Anette (*pale, with large eyes*): Georges!

Georges: Entre nous soit dit. Anette, you will suffer like the Virgin Mary when your boy goes to war. You will unbutton my naval coat, pin a gold medallion on me and you'll cry like my mother used to.

(Anette, visibly moved, opens her handbag.)

Georges: Outside, an evening like a sad monk and a star like a
    candle. My father will call me and taking off his glasses
    he'll say: Georges, be a faithful servant of the tsar . . . and
    not a word more.

(Anette takes out some banknotes.)

Georges: We'll ride quickly to the station. You'll be with me.
    Papa at the back. I'll enter a first-class carriage and will
    find there a beautiful, unknown, young woman, just like
    you, Anette. (*He kisses her.*) She will have round, white
    elbows and breasts like yours, Anette. It will be night;
    there will be a journey, talk and adventure. (*He kisses her
    passionately.*)

Anette (*both frightened and pleased*): Georges! I'll call papa!

Georges (*drawing back*): The engine will sigh and move in the
    direction of the front. Its whistle will sound: war, war. The
    Emperor, Russia, hurrah! I have left for the war.

8

*Georges rushes by me like the wind and knocks on Zinka's
door.*

Zinka: Who is it?

Georges: It's me. Can I see you?

Zinka: Why?

Georges: I've come. Don't you know why?

Zinka: Are you looking for a mother or have you lost your
    way?

Georges: I've come. . . . My father sent me. To collect the rent.
    Father said he'd evict you if you don't pay today.

Zinka (*resigned*): Well, come in, Mr. Landlord.

9

*Almost on tiptoe I approach the fateful door and stand in
front of it. The first wave of the brilliant* allegro molto *fades.*

She continues playing—the tone poem of a rebellious spirit, an eternal song of love. Suddenly she stops.

She: Ah, my father, with a ragged Ukrainian mustache and a white tuft of hair!

Father (*reading solemnly*): "The chronicle of the teacher of painting and calligraphy, Ivan Stepanovych Stupay-Stupanenko, a Ukrainian of Zaporozhian lineage."

She (*humorously*): Oh!

Father: And so! "Seventh of March, 1917, in Ukraine. A month ago I could not sleep at night, thinking all the time that the night was as big as Russia and Russia as big as the night and nothing was heard of our Ukraine. But today I read the declaration of our Central Rada:* to the Ukrainian people, the people of peasants, workers and all toilers. . . . After one month—what a change. I bless the revolution!"

She: I bless it, too.

Father: "Twenty seventh of March. I read that on Sunday a large Ukrainian meeting was held in Kiev. Hundreds, thousands, tens of thousands of Ukrainians swore before Shevchenko's picture not to lay down their hands until our Ukraine is restored to full freedom. I swear it, too!"

She: I do too. Not only on Shevchenko, but on your mustache and your gray tuft.

Father: "The thirtieth: I dreamt about the glorious Hetman of all Ukraine, Ivan Stepanovych Mazepa."**

She: So did I. He was driving a car and behind him the Zaporozhians were all on motorbikes.

Father: "The thirty first. The Bolsheviks write that there is no need for national boundaries. They are for internationalism. Does that mean that Ukraine has no boundaries? They should be ashamed of themselves."

She: Yes, they should.

Father: P.S. I must explain the whole problem to them and especially what Ukraine is. (*Writing*) It's essential.(*Reading*) "It's the first today. Tomorrow is Easter. I wonder if God

---

*The Central Rada, the supreme council of independent Ukraine in 1917, later the government of the national Ukrainian People's Republic.

**Ivan Mazepa, Hetman of Ukraine (1687-1709), sided with Charles XII of Sweden against Russia's Peter I.

is necessary to Ukraine now? I think, if necessary, then he must be our own Ukrainian God. Another one would betray us. Maryna has played some wonderful music the whole evening. It must be Ukrainian because I can hear in it how the Zaporozhians ride through the steppes seeking fortune for their Ukraine." Especially when she plays fast, like this—tam-tam-tam. (*He kisses her.*) Play it to me.

She plays. A wave of sounds rises to the starry skies. Behind it, the corner of the room seems to float under the taut sail of the curtain: Shevchenko's bust, the flowers, she, bent over the piano, her father with his chronicle and I, behind the door. We are like the Argonauts on a journey to wonderful lands, each in search of his own golden fleece.

Father: Is this a sonata?

She: *Sonata Pathetique.*

Father: Who wrote it?

She: Beethoven.

Father: Not a Ukrainian?

She: A German.

Father: Then his mother was Ukrainian.

She: Father, you are funny. The composer died a hundred years ago and never lived in Ukraine.

Father: He must have heard Ukrainian music. It's a Ukrainian sonata. The Russians stole Hlynka from us and say that he is their Glinka. He's not Glinka but Hlynka. A Ukrainian surname—he must be Ukrainian. But from now on, Maryna, we won't give up any Ukrainians. I plan to go out into the streets at once, to churches, wherever there are people and demonstrate in favor of a free Ukraine. Now every Ukrainian, before he goes to sleep, must think about Ukraine and must get up in the morning with his country as his chief concern. First, let's rebuild it and then we'll support internationalism. That's the way to do it, not the way you write about it, comrade Bolsheviks. How can internationalism exist without Ukraine, without the *bandura*?

Maryna: Father, you are funny. (*She kisses him.*)

Father: I'm going.

I shove the letter between the door and the doorpost and run upstairs to my room, feverish with expectancy.

10

Stupay (*having opened the door*): Maryna, here's a letter for you.

Maryna: Without a stamp or a postmark?

Stupay: It's a golden letter which falls into the laps of Ukrainian girls. (*He leaves.*)

Maryna (*alone*): Not a golden, but a naked one. (*She reads, repeating some words aloud.*) " . . . This music is certainly about a young man who rides on horseback through the steppes in search of a land of eternal love. . . ." (*With some amusement*) There you are! Here's another funny man. On a horse, I bet, in calico shorts. . . .(*Reading*)"There, at the blue window stands a lonely girl," Aha! (*She smiles and raises her eyebrow.*) "Tell me, winds or stars, will she come out to meet him. . . ." (*A pause.*) Tell me, winds, whisper to me, stars, how to answer such a funny man—the hermit in the attic? (*She sits down. A desk, a pencil. Her left hand is on the piano keyboard, her right hand is writing*): "The girl is lonely, yes. She is waiting. I do not know for whom but she has been waiting a long time. In her dreams and visions she has waited and still waits, as in the blue mists of past ages, for someone from behind the Dnieper, or from the three Cossack mounds, from the Zhovti Vody* or the Sich.** For whom? (*Touching the keyboard*) Perhaps for you, my dear poet. Certainly for you, if you are on a horse and armed." No, I can't write that—it sounds like program notes. Let me write from the heart. (*Playing a chord*) "A lonely girl waits for you, my poet. In the land of eternal love." No, that sounds like his letter. "In a land where there are two rusty bolts on a gate—one Muscovite and the other Polish. She waits and dreams that she will give her body and soul to the one who will smash these bolts." Let it come from the heart! . . .

---

*Zhovti Vody—the place where in the 17th century the Cossacks under Bohdan Khmelnytsky defeated the Poles.

**Sich—the stronghold of the Zaporozhian Cossacks.

11

Maryna is playing. I feel that in another second, in another chord, the wave of brilliant pathos will reach the sky and bounce off the stars, and then the sky, the piano, the silver horn of the moon will play a symphony pathetique over the entire world. I can see unbearably clearly, I can see the starry distance and I can hear the music of the spheres, but I cannot see Maryna carrying a letter to me. A soldier intercepts her on the stairs. He is an officer. He turns and runs to her enthusiastically:

Mon Dieu! Is it you, Marine? How are you? Do you recognize your old high school chevalier d'amour—André? I haven't seen you for three years. More! Do you remember I wrote a secret note to you at a dance where I met you? And how we danced the waltz and the minuet? You are even more beautiful now.

Maryna: Have you come from the front?

André: Just now. I am so happy. Imagine: darkness, trenches, clay, bog, day after day, month after month. A man turns into clay there and without a woman, without a soul, becomes a victim of a heavy oppressive urge. And now what a contrast, I ride in a train, there are city lights and Ukrainian stars.

Maryna: You are a Russian.

André: But I love them because they are mine. I ride in a train, there are lights and stars, a station and a coachman—what a devilish panorama. To top it all the bells are ringing and suddenly you appear, Marine, ma première tendresse. . . . I can't talk any more. (*With outstretched hands*) Well, Christ is Risen!

Maryna (*steps back*): Indeed, He is Risen!

André: Well then, let me kiss your shadow. (*Kissing her*) For this one moment, for this encounter I am ready to go back to the front and fight for a year without leave. All for your sake!

Maryna: And for the Ukrainian stars?

André: I am ready to fight against the whole world.

Maryna: Thank you. But you must visit your family first, wash and rest. That's an order.

André: Marine!

Maryna: Come to see us tomorrow.

The officer, kissing her with his eyes, runs home. Maryna goes in my direction. She comes to a halt. One step forward, one step back.

Maryna: A poet, perhaps, can conquer your soul and the whole world, but not a kilometer of any territory, my Jeanne d'Arc. (*She goes back.*)

12

For the third time I hear the Sonata Pathetique. *Suddenly the accompaniment to the* grave *resembles a fugue of Easter bells. I look out of the little window. Bellfries as tall as poplars. From the nearest one there comes a chorus: Christ is Risen! Cometlike the stars shine red, blue and green. The universe is in a swirl in this concert. Only low over the horizon there hangs under the crescent moon—the crucified Christ.*

13

Stupay comes back, excited and uplifted. His tuft of hair is ruffled.

Stupay: Maryna, play Sonata Pathetique.   Ukraine is rising from the dead. I have just got three more memberships in our reading circle: a school teacher, a carpenter from nearby and a night watchman. Play! Holy Russia, you daughter of a bitch, we'll kick your big fat backside now. Can you hear how Ukraine is playing and ringing? The gray-haired Zaporozhians are rising from their graves and saddling their horses again. Can you hear them riding?

Maryna (*plays*): You won't win with any help from the grave. Father, we need partisans, youth!

Stupay: They are racing across the Ukrainian steppes in search of a golden destiny. They are flying over the ages, brandishing their spears!

Maryna: Instead of your dreams, father, we need cannons and machine guns!

Stupay: What?

Maryna: Never mind, father. You're a poet.

Stupay: I am a Ukrainian. Wait, Maryna. I'm going to exchange Easter greetings with them. (*He picks up the telephone.*) Please give me 23-07. Is that the school principal? Ivan Stepanovych Stupay-Stupanenko wishes you a Happy Easter. Ukraine has risen! What do you say to that? Indeed she has risen! Ha! Play, Maryna! Please give me 17-00. I wish to speak to Major-General Perotsky!

14

Perotsky, wearing a uniform, near the telephone.

Perotsky: With whom do I have the honor?

Stupay: A Ukrainian, Ivan Stepanovych Stupay-Stupanenko, wants to wish you a Happy Easter. Ukraine has risen, your excellency!

Perotsky (*waiting till his heart beats more quietly, then answering in Russian*): My reply is: Attention! Take your right marker, Ukrainians, on the one-and-indivisible Russia!

Stupay: It's different in Ukrainian, your excellency. Attention! A Russian general out of Ukraine, quick march! Maryna, play the *Pathetique*!

15

Zinka (*reading*): "This receipt is issued to our former chamber maid, Zinaida Masiukova, to certify that on the orders of my father, General Perotsky, I received from her the sum of seven rubles as rent and also on my father's orders I returned the money to her in compensation for my first visit to her and in addition paid her seven more rubles which my father owed her for his visit on Easter, 1913. Signed: graduate of the cadet officer corps, Georges Perotsky." So now you can go home.

Georges (*kneeling*): Tear it up, please, tear it up. At least promise not to show it to anyone.

Zinka (*shows him out, closes the door. Alone*): Oh, God, how difficult it is. (*She takes a guitar, plays and prays at the same time.*) God, dear God, why don't you help me? Perhaps you don't want to? . . .

16

In the basement Nastia stands like a statue. In the doorway crawls a legless soldier wearing the ribbon of the St. George Cross.

Do you recognize your husband, Nastia? Hallo! As you can see, they've shortened me a bit, made me lower than anyone else. But it does not matter. I'll go back to the comrades in the factory, they'll lift me up. I'll crawl but I'll get there. For two months I've been crawling back to you. Why are you staring? Come and let me put my arms around you, though I'm only half of your husband. (*He crawls to the middle of the basement and cries.*)

ACT TWO

1

Daytime. The helicon gleams in the sun. After a sleepless night I walk tirelessly up and down in my room. Underneath the clock strikes from time to time. Maryna is playing the same Sonata Pathetique, *but today I can't hear the starry* grave *or the brilliant* allegro, *but the gay* adagio cantabile *like flowers in the sun. As usual, I can visualize a limitless steppe and above, in the Argonaut boat, she floats, with her left eyebrow raised, her eyes deep blue, and there are flowers and dew on the oars. And then, for the second time, I am visited by my unromantic friend, Luka:*

Did you get there?

(I, pretending not to understand, remain silent.)

Luka (*maliciously*): To her gates?

(I remain silent.)

Luka: I bet you tore up your letter.

I (*in an ecstasy*): I delivered it, I swear I did.

Luka (*taken aback*): Well, and what happened?

I: Guess: what's the way the world has inevitably followed for thousands of years?

Luka (*having understood that I am hopelessly in love, with grim determination*): The way of revolution!

I: The way of love! Guess, Luka, without what would the world have long ago wandered like a eunuch across the desert of life?

Luka: Without the way of revolution, just as you are now wandering like a eunuch right here. Listen, Ilko! Today there's a demonstration at eleven. The organizers are all those who turn a revolution into an operetta or a liturgy and the class struggle into a parade. So at least our

57

comrade from Petrograd has told us. I agree with him. I bet your Ukrainians will join them, all decked out in embroidered shirts. The Bolsheviks are staging a counter-demonstration. Do you understand? The workers in our factory are all pro-Bolshevik. I was asked to distribute literature on our street and to canvass against the war, for an eight-hour working day and for a subscription to "Pravda." Well, let's go. You can help to distribute literature. In any case there'll be more of us out there.

I: I can't go.

Luka: Why?

I: I . . . I'm going to see her right now. You don't believe me? I would have gone long ago, but two wild beasts were holding me back: shyness and misanthropy. After a sleepless night I've tamed them and while they sleep I'll go. At once! I've prepared in my mind the opening words for our encounter: "Don't be surprised," I will say, "that I come univited—it is you who have entered my heart without an invitation." No, that's wrong. I'll simply say: "How are you? I've come without an invitation; this is a privilege of old men and lovers."

Luka: No, you had better say this: "Are you by yourself? Because I am not myself. I've come so that you can see an idiot with an icon of eternal love around his neck, tied to a girl's apronstrings rather than to the red flag. I'm an idiot, an idler and a traitor." That's all. And you had better realize, Ilko, that I've come to you for the last time and for the last time I'm telling you: we wrote verses together, you taught me arithmetic and geography, we read books together and we were friends, but if you won't come out into the street now and choose the path of revolution, I'm no longer your friend, and you aren't mine. One! Two! Three! (*He goes.*)

I (*after him*): Luka, you must admit it's easier to stir up three revolutions at once than tell a girl that you love her. What? You see, I'm going.

Indeed I go downstairs. One current carries me to her doors, the other diverts me and pushes me down.

Unheard conversation.

Maryna (*finishing playing*): Enough!

André: Marine, more, more!

Maryna: You like it, too?

André (*jealously*): Why too? Who else likes it?

Maryna: Guess.

André: Oh yes, of course he does.

Maryna: That's right. Last night he even woke me up (*André's eyes pop out*) and said: "Daughter, play the *Pathetique* because I can't sleep."

André: I'd wake you too, if I were with you.

Maryna: He always dreams when he hears this music—about the Zaporozhians, the steppes, Ukraine. And what do you dream about?

André: I . . . guess!

Maryna: Russia?

André: I honor it but I don't dream about it.

Maryna: Revolution?

André: I welcome it but I have no dreams about it.

Maryna: Surely not Ukraine?

André: Ukrainian stars and bells. I am walking along. A sudden meeting. I kiss her shadow. I want to pick her up and carry her in my arms.

Maryna: You said you welcomed the revolution. What for?

André: What we need now is a three-cornered hat rather than Monomakh's furcap.*

Maryna: And guess what I dream about when I listen to this music?

---

*André favors a military dictatorship over tsarist autocracy.

59

André: Your father?

Maryna: Something wonderful and unintelligible. Vision, dream and reality all merge into one. The country is dark and wild, so oppressed that it has even forgotten its history and doesn't know what will happen to it tomorrow. The dream: two rusty locks hang on a gate, one with a white and the other with a two-headed eagle.* The past and the future are locked. There is a lonely girl in this dark country. She dreams and waits. Do you know for whom?

André: For whom?

Maryna: A knight who loves Ukrainian stars.

André: Really?

Maryna: Day after day, night after night I wait for him to come and break these locks and open the gate. . . .

André: For the girl?

Maryna: For the girl and for the country. (*She plays a few chords on the piano and lifts them in her hands like flowers.*) My dreams of love are a vision of this girl meeting her knight. (*She looks as if she were in love, like the girl in her dream.*) My darling, my long awaited one! . . . She will lead him, like a Hetman, into her living room. And she will say: let the bells of St. Sophia ring out so that people won't hear me kissing my lover. . . .

André: Marine! Tell me! Is this only a dream or is there a way to realize it, a practical program?

Maryna: This is just a dream, the musical vision of a whimsical girl. But, then, instead of a three-cornered hat can there be a Hetman's mace? If so, then this is a program for Ukraine. You are forming Cossack partisan units and I am organizing this movement. This is a practical way. Something strange and unintelligible—isn't it?

André: Let the girl wait for her knight.

Maryna: Yes?

André: The knight will come. He is on the threshold. . . .

---

*While the eagle is the national emblem of Poland, a two-headed eagle is that of tsarist Russia.

I open the door quietly:

Excuse me! I came uninvited—it is the privilege of old men and lovers. . . .
I can see the officer's back. He is kneeling down and kissing the hem of her dress. "The knight is here, Marinon. He asks your blessing, darling." I hear this and, unnoticed, go away.

5

I return to my attic. I am unbearably depressed. I cannot recognize objects. Everything has changed, grown dimmer and darker. Even the sun does not look like the sun, but like a yellow plaster on a wound. I whisper in agony:

What does it matter? Remember when you were still a little boy, you chased dreams on a hobbyhorse and sometimes fell off and cut your bare foot on a sharp broken glass till the piercing ache reached your heart? Remember how you fell off the hobbyhorse into some garbage? That's what it is now—garbage around you and you fell off your visionary horse. Is our world a garbage dump, and do dreams rise from it like vapors? Yes, Luka, all our paths in this world are merely orbits. It doesn't matter which you take, you will go back where you started from—a hole. The difference is that when you are born you fall out of a hole, when you die you fall into a hole. That's all. Where shall I go? Try another orbit? (*I approach the window.*) Shall I jump down, or what? (*I look around aimlessly.*)

ACT THREE

1

Imagine, my friends, a street in an old provincial city, a sunny building on a corner, a cloud over the golden-domed cathedral and the distant sound of the Marseillaise. A bootblack, sitting down, is singing:

> On Saturdays and Sundays,
> Day after day,
> Men in boots
> Used to prowl
> Down city streets.
>
> But now freedom has come,
> The street's not the same,
> There's no work for anyone
> From Sunday to this day.

2

Another bootblack comes up and sits down:

Bravo, bravo! You're like a singer who sings while the opera house is burning.

First: Do you have a ticket allowing you to occupy this spot? Off with you!

Second: Don't start thinking that this is an opera and you are at the ticket office.

First: This is my place.

Second: Now there is freedom of speech, conscience and place.

First: They write: "Proletarians of all countries unite" and what about you?

Second: I've come to unite.

First (*singing and drumming with his brushes*):

> I clean and I clean —
> Those boots shine like the sun.

Second (*louder*):

> And I shall clean the sun
> Better than boots.

First: So you come here to compete? Get out, I say!

Second: Pst! Quiet! See, there's our real competitor (*points to Ovram*).

3

Ovram crawls up carrying a bag with brushes.

Second: There's a wartime proverb: when two fight, the third should keep out. Isn't that the truth, comrade soldier?

Ovram: The war is over for me, that's why I am crawling.

Second: You're crawling to a place where there's no more work to be done than polishing one's own boots.

Ovram: How I wish I had a job like that. Then I wouldn't have to crawl.

4

I see the street filling up with people. The sound of the Marseillaise grows louder. A cloud floats from the cathedral. Old Perotsky comes out onto the balcony. Maryna and André stand on a lower balcony.

Maryna: See what a wonderful day it is. It will be a day like this, sent by the heavens, when the girl meets her knight. (*Checking André's movement towards her.*) Pst. Look down, there's my father going to canvass. Let's listen. He's really funny, with a blue and yellow flower* in his buttonhole! . . .

The First Bootblack (*meeting Stupay*):

> I clean and I clean —
> This boot polish is like freedom.

Second:

> See how the sun shines,
> That's because of my work.

Stupay (*putting his leg in front of the first bootblack*): Go ahead and clean. But wait a moment. Who are you?

First: What do you mean who? A bootblack. (*A crowd gathers.*)

Stupay: Not that. What nationality are you?

First: I am a citizen of the Russian state.

Perotsky (*on the balcony*): Bravo!

Stupay (*withdrawing his foot and putting it in front of the second bootblack*): And what nationality are you?

Second: Whatever you like.

Stupay (*to Ovram*): And you? (*Recognizing him*) Ah, our neighbor from below, Ovram Kotlar. One of us, a Ukrainian! Go ahead and clean my boots (*puts his shoe in front of him*).

Maryna (*on the balcony, to Andrê*): Isn't he funny?

Andrê: That's a good example for us. I approve.

Second (*to the first bootblack*): Have you ever seen anyone so crazy?

First: What does he want?

Second: He wants the nation to clean his shoes.

Stupay: We, Stupay-Stupanenkos don't want our nation to clean foreign shoes. Enough of that! It's time to be free! Let's ride our horses and race across the steppes with the eagles and the winds. (*He can almost hear the sound of horses' hooves as an echo of the* Pathetique.)

Maryna: Bravo, father, bravo!

Andrê: Bravo!

Ovram: You may be all right, but what are you going to do about us?

Stupay: About whom?

---

*Blue and yellow are the national colors of Ukraine.

Ovram: About me—a legless Ukrainian proletarian (*pointing to the bootblacks*) and about them?

Zinka (*comes out of the crowd, a little tipsy*): And what about me? Back under the saddle or on the mattress? (*To the crowd*) They told me when freedom came it would be like your own mother. Don't worry, girl, you'll be out of trouble. Life will be like a bed of roses, and your boyfriend will shine like the sun. Now I'm asking you: Where is my boy?

A voice from the crowd: Who?

Zinka: Whoever answers! (*Laughter*) Although they say I only charge five rubles I haven't sold out everything. I've kept something for the day when my boyfriend comes to me. That will be my Easter Day.

Laughter and voices: Millions will answer your call.

Zinka: Although there are millions of you, he's not one of you. I lit a candle and put on my blue dress, but he hasn't come. Then I thought I'd go to see a neighbor who's unhappy too. But he keeps writing letters. Then I decided to go out into the street to look for my beloved.

Perotsky (*from the balcony*): There's your freedom of speech, gentlemen! A symbol of your freedom!

Luka: Yes! That's the essence of bourgeois freedom. A pleading human being. (*To the crowd*) Comrades!

André (*interrupting*): Citizens!

Stupay (*gathering up his wits*): Fellow Ukrainians!
I can see three currents flowing through the crowd. Each wants to gather round its orator. André is given an ovation. That's why he begins to speak first:
Who hasn't seen, who hasn't known our land of yesterday. Our country. . . .

Stupay: Ukraine!

Luka: The working people, the proletariat!

André: The whole of Russia was a stagnant and oppressive monument. The steps leading up to the throne footholds for us slaves. The golden collars, senators, court councillors—they were all tyrants.

Luka: Comrades! That's a lie! We were and we are slaves—workers, soldiers, Russians and others! . . .

Stupay: There are no slaves more wretched than the Ukrainians.

André: Both peasants and Ukrainians were slaves. Citizens! This land of slavery and oppression. . . .

Stupay: Ukraine!

André: This country of obscurantism and prose. . . .

Luka: Of crosses and gallows. . . .

André: This country I couldn't see through my tears. (*With pathos*) And today?

He pauses, and the normal, matter-of-fact voice of the bootblack is heard:

Shoeshine, gentlemen!

André: And today we can see and we can smell the wide road to freedom. Those shining horizons, yes! We should saddle horses and race to the west and to the east. So that our country may be borne not by a troyka, but by a million steel horses, so that the Dardanelles will fall into ruins before them and so that all nations and states must let us pass and the winds and distant horizons greet us!

Applause. Shouts of "Glory." Noise.

A Young Girl (*enthusiastically to a sailor*): So now you're going to pierce the Dardanelles?

Sailor (*with one eye missing, pock-marked and with a voice like a broken down accordion*): Your Dardanelles, Miss, we'll pierce now, if you like, but let them (*pointing to André*) crack the Turkish ones.

A Lady (*feathers in her hat shake belligerently*): At our meeting we, the weaker sex, have rejected the proposal to stop the war. We said: we are not fighting against the German people but against the Kaiser. Forward! To the front!

Sailor (*makes way for her*): Please go first!

Luka: Instead of the golden Hetman's mace may the mace of proletarian dictatorship shine in Ukraine!

Sailor: Down with the bourgeoisie!

André: Our platform is: liberty, equality, fraternity!

Young Girl (*whose shoes are being cleaned by Ovram*): Liberty, equality, fraternity. (*She stamps her foot in excitement.*)

Ovram (*throwing his shoecleaning box down*): For ten years I worked in a factory and for three years I was at the front. For that, as you see, they gave me a medal. Now they offer me freedom—to crawl with my medal into the grave. Liberty? I have no bread. Equality? I am lower than everyone else without my legs. Fraternity? I clean your shoes. Take your medal and give me back my legs. (*He throws down his St. George Cross.*)

Luka: Our platform: All power to the Soviets! World revolution! Socialism!

Georges stands on the roof of the building, holding the Russian flag. He is without a cap. He cries enthusiastically:
Long live Russia and the Emperor!
Then he shoots. I can see Luka falter. I call out: Luka! and run quickly downstairs. On the street I see people scattering in all directions. The place is deserted except for Luka who is wounded in the arm, Zinka who is bandaging him, Ovram, and the sailor, who swears:
You just wait, you just wait. Your time will come too!

ACT FOUR

1

Imagine, my friends, the same street and town late in October. Artillery firing is heard in the distance. A windy night. I stand guard at the secret Red partisan point situated in Ovram's room in the basement.

2

The window in the basement is shut. An oil lamp flickers. Water drips from the ceiling. Hamar is writing. He is wearing a cap. Next to him a partisan, also in a cap, waits impatiently. Ovram sits in the corner; next to him, like a shadow, Nastia.

Hamar: To the Revolutionary HQ. . . (*He stops to think and tears up what he has written.*) No, better go and tell them. The position is as follows: the railway station is in the hands of the partisans—they all seem to be pro-Bolshevik. The Whites are on this side. Their reserves are close by—they are about three hundred men, armed with machine guns. They are in an angry mood and they are hanging people. They are praying for victory too. We are scattered in various buildings in threes and fives. Altogether about 70 workers. All ready to fight. But we have very few arms. Three bullets per rifle. Yet we are all full of enthusiasm. Still, I think it's dangerous to start an uprising without some understanding with the partisans. I've sent Luka to contact them and I'm waiting for his return. If he doesn't

68

come back, we have agreed to start the fight before moonrise. That's all.

Nastia: Someone's coming. . . .

Ovram (*after a while*): It's the wind.

Hamar (*wrapped in his own thoughts*): What?

Ovram: The wind!

Hamar looks at his watch.

Nastia: The seven-hundred-and-fifth drop has fallen since he went. Sixth, seventh, eighth. . . .

Ovram: Quiet!

The messenger sets off.

3

In the meantime, upstairs—

Maryna (*writing*): "HQ. To André Perotsky. . . ." (*She tears up what she has written and turns to her father.*) You'd better go and tell them.

Stupay: Perhaps we could phone?

Maryna: Funny! These matters aren't discussed on the phone. Tell them that the committee. . . .

Stupay: What kind of committee is this, Maryna?

Maryna: He'll know. . . . At the moment we can't give any assistance. But the committee is trying to organize village detachments. Tell them in one more day they'll get some help. What else? That there is unrest in our basement—he knows that. But tell them: there is a possibility of a workers' uprising. We must beware of a blow from the rear. Tell them that. Go and run, my dear, and find out what the feeling is at the front and at HQ. That's all. (*She kisses him.*)

Stupay: Running again! I don't know whether I'm a Ukrainian of Zaporozhian descent or a horse. I don't understand anything. Some committee. There should be a military council, not a committee. That's not the way the Zaporozhians fought. (*He runs out.*)

4

I signal to my friends: "danger" and hide behind a balustrade. An enemy patrol walks along the street. Two of them are furtively smoking. Their mustaches glow and their badges flash. One of them trips.

First Soldier: What the hell! (*Sotto voce*) They buried him but his feet are sticking out below the knees.

Second: You aren't sorry, are you? Those are Bolshevik legs!

First: I'm not sorry, but you can trip over them if we have to run.

Third (*appears to be drunk, stopping in front of the body*): How striking and original! My opposite! His head down, my head up. When it's day for us, it's night for him and vice versa. What strange geography! Let's urinate on him!

5

At times I think I can hear someone playing. But, surely, this is because of tension. My ear cannot be trusted. It may not be my ear, but the wind in the wires. Yes, that's it. Who else would dare to play on such a night. Only the wind. Or perhaps a drunken Zinka is playing the guitar— she was having a good time with some officers today. But what if it isn't the wind or Zinka, but someone else? What if it is she? Her window is covered with a thick tapestry. Perhaps a candle is burning. It is as quiet as in a cabin, only dull artillery fire can be heard in the distance. She is restless. She is listening and walking quietly. Now she is trying to play even more quietly the rondo *from the* Pathetique. *Yes, she is playing. Let her boat, full of music, float in the middle of this anxious black night, disturbed by the wind.*

6

I feel strange: I stand on guard, but all around me music flows. A yellowish streak of light flashes somewhere (Maryna lifts the edge of the tapestry in the window) and disappears with a blue afterglow. It is swept away by the wind and the music of the Pathetique *(she moves away from the window and plays the* grave). *Behind the bass chords horses' hooves can be heard. Someone is making a fire. A horse is racing through the dark steppe. That is me, racing on a horse into the land of eternal love! Behind the black horizon, near the blue window she is waiting for me, looking out for me. (Now Maryna once again uncovers the window and looks out. She is going downstairs to meet me.) She is stretching out her hands, her left eyebrow is a little raised and her eyes are smiling. (She looks at me in my sleep.) We are engulfed by the music of the* rondo. *It is a silvery serpentine melody. At the same time I can feel the wind and see the night. "The sun doesn't love the earth as much as I love you," I want to say it to Maryna, but I cannot. She, as it were, moves away, floats away. The serpentine melody is broken and is carried away by the wind. She seems to be in a boat. I see the mast, the billowing sail, the taut ropes. Instead of the* rondo *I hear once more the* grave. *Maryna stands under the sail.*

—Is this the Argo?, I ask.

—This is an old Zaporozhian boat, she answers.

—Cossack boats had no sails, I mention.

—This is not a sail!

I look and see a flag, a yellow and blue one. We sail off. Luka comes to meet us. Bent over, he carries a red banner on his back. For some reason it is as round as the moon. I remember that I left my guard post, that to him I am a traitor. I am overcome with shame, restlessness, and fear.

Luka!, I cry out.

Quiet!, admonishes Luka.

7

Indeed, it is Luka who, bending down, runs across the street. The moon is visible on the horizon. It is deep red and wind-blown and resembles a flag.

I (*to Luka*): Well?

Luka (*out of breath*): Oh, this moonlight! Faster! Where is Hamar?

I: Here!

Hamar meets us on the steps.

Luka (*agitated*): I ran through the cemetery, down the gulley. (*To me*) Remember that's where we used to go for walks, where you taught me to write verse. The Whites didn't see me, but the partisans almost shot me. They thought I was a spy. At last their commander stopped me and asked who and how strong we were. I told him—we are workers, we lack arms. I told him everything. They said this to me: as soon as the moon rises we should attack from the rear, then they will attack as well. I ran as fast as I could because the moon is already rising. (*To me*) And this devilish wind. . . .

Hamar (*enthusiastically*): It is our moon and the wind is on our side. Wait a little longer—the whole world will be ours. Let them put up gallows, crosses. . . .

Nastia (*listening*): They are singing "Our Father". . . .

Hamar: Let them say their prayers and sing "Our Father"! The world, my friends, will be ours! We shall make triumphal arches out of the gallows. We'll take the crosses and bury them, along with capitalism, in cemeteries. We will march forward to the dawn of socialism! (*To me*) You must go to HQ. Tell them that we are starting. . . .(*Fixes his cap more firmly on his head*) Give them our greetings! (*To Luka*) You will show the partisans the way during the battle. Well. . . . (*He hesitates whether to say goodbye.*)

Nastia: Perhaps we should all sit down according to the old custom?

Ovram: I'd like to be able to stand up. Well, give my greetings to all of them—the whole proletariat! (*Through tears*) But take care of your legs, brothers. The legs! (*Calming down*) But then, (*smiling*) the main thing is not to lose your head, never mind your legs. (*He notices that Luka's shoes are all in tatters.*) Nastia, get him my boots. Let them go into attack on another man's legs.

(*Hiding behind the stove, Nastia takes off her own boots and gives them to Luka.*)

Luka (*takes them*): I'll change on the way.

We are silently climbing the steps. The wind hits our faces. The moon is rising. Before parting, Luka and I romantically shake hands.

I (*uplifted*): The world, Luka, will be ours! . . .

Luka: It certainly will! (*After I leave he speaks alone.*) Should I take these boots or not? It's true there are puddles on the way, but Nastia will be without boots. And they will be pulled off me if I am killed. Let them stay. (*He puts them under the door and runs.*)

Nastia (*after a pause*): They've gone. Will they come back before dawn, Ovram?

Ovram is silent. The water drips.

Nastia (*out of habit*): One, two, three. . . .

8

Stupay returns. He stops at the half-buried body, shakes his head and runs to his apartment.

Maryna (*anxiously coming up to her father*): Did you pass the message?

Stupay: Yes.

Maryna: Well, how is it there?

Stupay: The moon is rising.

Maryna: Oh, God! He's on about the moon.

Stupay: And the wind! Maryna, do you hear?

Maryna (*ironically*): From the south?

Stupay: From the north.

Maryna: A pity. We need a western wind. Are the stars out?

Stupay (*realizing her irony*): The wind is straight from the front. From the partisans. (*Almost with enthusiasm*) They say there are many Ukrainians among them. (*Seeing Maryna's interest in it*) Almost all of them are Ukrainians.

Maryna: And do they themselves know they are Ukrainians?

Stupay: Hm! (*After a pause*) As a matter of fact, only a few of them are Ukrainians. At the HQ I heard no Ukrainian spoken. Some people are hostile to it. Four out of five who were hanged were Ukrainians. The one who lies half-buried was a Ukrainian on his mother's side. He's already lost one boot. But not a word about Ukraine. Perhaps the red flag is better after all, Maryna?

Maryna: Even if our yoke turns red it will still be a yoke. (*Stupay sighs.*) Have you seen anyone apart from the moon?

Stupay: Yes, I did.

Maryna: And have you heard anyone apart from the wind?

Stupay: Yes, I have.

Maryna: Well?

Stupay (*after a pause*): It seems that they can't hold out. They are ready to flee.

Maryna (*upset*): Really? (*She telephones.*) HQ? Please call Ensign Perotsky to the phone. . . .

9

General Perotsky (*at the phone, Anette holds a candle*): HQ? Please call Ensign Perotsky. André—is that you? Why is there no electricity? Besides, Georges has fled from home. Most probably to the front. He asked Anette to give him the golden medallion with the Virgin Mary. He took a rifle too. For God's sake find him and force him to come back home. For God's sake! How are things at the front? I'm calm, but I had a dream: Russia was like a deserted field with a stove and an icon in the middle. Then Stupay comes and sits on the stove. What arrogance! (*He is upset.*) Do you hear, André? André? (*Artillery barrage grows louder. Anette drops the candle. Perotsky is in the dark.*) HQ? The telephone has been disconnected. (*Anette uncovers the window. The red moon in the sky casts a reflection in the mirror. Perotsky shouts.*) Cover the window!

74

10

Nastia (*before the gunshot*): Tenth, eleventh, twelfth. (*Gunshot.*)
Ovram (*loudly*): The last one! Open the door!
Nastia: For whom?
Ovram (*his voice raised*): For whom? For the socialist revolution!

11

Stupay (*tries to uncover the window*): I'll go to meet them!
Maryna: They'll kill you.
Stupay: I have arms.
Maryna: What arms?
Stupay: The Ukrainian language.
Maryna: A language is only persuasive when it's backed by weapons.
Stupay: I will meet them and remind them of Shevchenko's sacred words: "Embrace, my brethren, the smallest one."
Maryna: Who will you remind of it? The Bolsheviks? The bandits? The bloodthirsty barbarians who are destroying our loftiest ideals? (*She covers the window.*)

12

Along the street the Whites are fleeting, in groups and individually. Someone again trips over the legs of the half-buried man and swears. There is a feeling of desolation. There are no lights in the windows, no voices in the street. Distant firing is heard. Moon. Wind.

13

Three crouching partisans run from shadow to shadow. The first is a sailor, the second wears a cap with a red band, the third one a fur jacket. They see the legs of the half-buried man and come closer.

Sailor (*blind in one eye, with a voice like an old accordion*): You can see by his legs that he fell in an unequal battle. (*After a pause*) Once you kill somebody you might just as well bury him. A man is not a cigarette butt to be stuck in the earth like that. To hell with that kind of civilization! (*He looks at the building.*) Perhaps we should turn this house into a coffin? Whoever is with us—follow me!
They march off with their rifles at the ready.

14

Ovram crawls out of the basement. The partisans have retreated. The sailor is asking Ovram with bitter humor:

Are these your legs, mate?
Ovram: Mine are in the ground. Imperialism has buried them.
Sailor: And these are half-buried by the bourgeoisie.
Ovram: Yes!
Sailor: So there isn't much difference between them.
Ovram (*crawls to the legs and inspects one boot*): Only one size different. (*His head droops.*)
Sailor: Down with the bourgeoisie!

15

They come to Stupay's door. The sailor tries to open it. It is unlocked and he throws it wide open:

Prepare yourselves for death.

Maryna (*calmly*): And my father wanted to go and meet you.
Sailor (*looking around*): Who is your father?
Stupay: A Ukrainian.
Sailor: That's pro forma. But who are you in your heart?
Stupay: A Ukrainian.
Maryna (*quietly*): In his heart he is a teacher.
Sailor (*goes out sullenly. Turning to the comrade in the fur cap*): Intellectuals. The door was open. Tell the others to leave them alone!
Comrade in a fur cap (*loudly so that he can be heard downstairs*): Tell the others—these are intellectuals—don't bother them!

16

They go further upstairs. The sailor reads the copper plate with Perotsky's name. He reads it slowly, syllable by syllable. Suddenly he turns to the others:

Halt! (*In a whisper*) Major-General Perotsky. Here's a class enemy, mates! (*Places his ear to the door*) I think there are two of them. (*He knocks quietly.*)
Anette: Don't go!
Perotsky (*quietly*): Perhaps it's Georges? Or André? (*He listens intently and puts his hand over Anette's watch.*) Who is it?
Sailor: Fate!
Comrade in the fur cap (*can no longer restrain himself, loudly*): Your fate! Open up! (*The sailor tries to quiet him down.*)
Anette: One moment. I'll find the key. (*To Perotsky*) We must flee! To Russia!
Perotsky: To Russia from Russia? Does this mean there is no Russia? (*Follows Anette to the back door. Soon after that the partisans break down the door.*)
Sailor: Mates, it looks as though he's run away from his fate. (*He searches the room.*)

17

Stupay's apartment.

Stupay: No! I think I am for socialism!

Maryna (*uncomprehending*): What do you mean?

Stupay: At least he talked to me in Ukrainian. A simple sailor. General Perotsky would sooner commit suicide than say a word in Ukrainian. No, the best ally is the one who uses Ukrainian.

Maryna: The best ally is the one whose arms support the Ukrainian cause.

Stupay: In a word, I am for socialism!

Maryna: You are funny!

Stupay: I am for socialism. Let the winds blow, even if they are from the north, as long as they sweep through our Cossack steppes.

Maryna: Whom should they sweep out?

Stupay: The Perotskys, for instance. I'd help the wind myself to get rid of them. (*He begins to blow.*)

18

Perotsky is on the doorstep:

Excuse me, but the partisans are after me. I am in flight. May I come in?

Stupay (*angrily*): It's high time you took to flight.

Perotsky: May I come here?

Stupay: Here?

There is the sound of a door falling down under the blows of riflebutts.

Voice of the sailor: He's fled—our principal enemy! Search for him. Don't let him get away!

Voice of the comrade in fur cap: Put the sentries on every door!

Perotsky: I am fleeing from death. May I come in?

Stupay (*hesitating*): Yes, do.

Maryna (*to Perotsky*): Where is André?

Perotsky: I don't know. Everything is lost!

Maryna is ready to go. She ties a kerchief round her hair and looks into a mirror.

19

A guard is placed at the entry to Perotsky's building. Fires burn in the street. Two men are leading Andrė. He is without his cap.

First guard: Is comrade Fate here?

Second guard: Yes. What happened?

First guard: We've brought a prisoner.

Second guard: Where from?

First guard: He says he's fled from the Whites and knows a secret.

Second guard (*looking at Andrė*): Watch out, citizen. Don't try to fool comrade Fate. (*Andrė is taken away.*)

20

Knocking on Stupay's door. Maryna opens it.

Guard: Where is comrade Fate who is in charge?

Maryna: He's upstairs, in the general's apartment. I will take you there. (*She shows him the way.*) Your commander is searching for the general who fled. Do you, by any chance, know comrade Yuha?

Guard: No, I haven't heard that name.

Maryna: A pity, he is on the Bolshevik side too. I'll search for him and send him to you.

21

I come up to the guard:

Can you tell me where the commandant of the partisan detachment is? (*The guard silently and suspiciously looks at me.*) Where can I find comrade Fate?

Guard: You are very curious. Who are you?

I: I am a messenger from HQ, from Hamar. (*I show him a small parcel. They show me the way up.*)

22

I pass a sentry and walk upstairs. Suddenly I hear "Excuse me." I turn back and see her. Quite close. Almost too close, so I stand back. I feel the Sonata Pathetique *race through my blood with its enchanting chords. Her eyes are azure-blue.*

She: We should meet among flowers, but, as a matter of fact, I want to ask you a favor. (*I listen to her voice and remain silent.*) Could I lay it on your triumphal path? (*Quite stupidly I continue my silence.*) It won't delay you long. You can step around it and go on or trample it and still go on.

I: What if I pick it up?

She: If you do, then bring it to the poet who wrote a letter to me. Is he still alive?

I: Alive.

She: Is he still racing on horseback through the steppe and asking the wind where to go? Has he forgotten about the girl?

I: I have not forgotten and never will forget. But he raced on a hobbyhorse and lived on dreams. He lived in the past. Now he wants to live in the future, so he is changing horses.

She: Which is his horse now?

I: The one with the flaming mane. The horse of revolution.

She: Tell him that a lonely Ukrainian girl is waiting for him near the water-well. Will he make a detour, if only for one hour, to see her?

I: Yes!

She: Tell him that the girl is waiting for him. But she is not alone. Her old mother is with her. She is waiting for her sons to return from the war on black, Cossack horses. . . .

I: Those horses are in a museum.

She (*flaring up*): Our horses are locked up by foreign powers. They are neighing. They want to get loose. Don't you hear them? Is the most sacred idea of national liberation alien to you?

I: I am for it, but. . . .

She: There is no "but." Have the glorious Cossack banners of Bohdan, Doroshenko, Mazepa, Kalnysh and Honta utterly faded for you? (*A pause.*)

23

Two men pass us. One of them boasts:

I'm for internationalism, Mykesha. I am for all the languages, you know, because I want to learn them all.

Mykesha: Such as?

The First One: Words like: Grand Hotel, agrarian, nationalization, proletariat—these are international.

24

She: Are you in favor of internationalism too?

I: Yes, I am. Are you?

She: I'm not against it. But I know too that ideas can only be victorious if the people who hold them are ready to go to the gallows and face death. What about your people?

I (*quietly*): They will face it.

She: Who, this riff raff and mob? One setback and they'll scatter to the four winds, will drop the idea in the mud along with their soldiers' caps and trample on it. All they

81

can do is kill unarmed people, put the gallows in every home!

I: But they don't bury living people, only dead ones.

She: Forgive me, but that was not what I was going to tell you. Not that at all! Nothing about politics, but something quite different. Something more important, human and simple. All of us looked out of the windows, when we were children, and hoped that the world would be bright and warm. As simple and intelligible as daylight, as our school primer. We cried over the body of a frozen bird. But now we are stepping over human corpses and we can't tell which of us is colder—the corpses or ourselves. Love, where have you gone from this world? Are you a dream? (*After a pause*) Tell me, does the poet still believe in Petrarch and eternal love?

I: Yes, that is his dream. And yours?

She: I will tell him about the girl who trusted the poet. She still trusts him and guards her love for him.

I (*music rises to the skies and I look into her blue eyes*): God! And you said you wanted a favor! This is such a joy, the greatest in my entire life!

She: I still have to ask you a favor—it's difficult for you and for me.

I: It's all the same to me. I will do it joyfully!

She: We must liberate André Perotsky! (*It is dark. I draw back and remain silent.*) I know it's difficult. But his corpse will fall across your path. And the path which leads from me to you. Neither you nor I wanted him to come between us. But it happened that way. I can't allow his corpse to separate us. He must be kept alive. Can't you possibly do it?

I: Do what?

She: Step over him to me?

I (*hoarsely*): I'll try.

She: What?

I: I'll try to rescue him.

25

*I go to the Perotsky apartment. The door is wide open. A
fresh wind rushes in from the street and threatens to blow
out the flames of three candles (one of them on the
window sill). I can see people's backs, caps, red bands,
rifles and smoke. André is being tried. He is capless. His
face is superficially calm, but inside it cries out with the
premonition of death.*

Sailor: What's your name?

André: Andrew.

Sailor: Last name?

André: Anon.

Sailor: Rank?

André: Officer-cadet in the reserve.

Sailor: Boys, you go on interrogating him. I can't carry on
because I know he's lying.

Partisan in a fur cap: Why did you join the cadets?

André: I was called up.

Partisan in a fur cap: I can't carry on, either.

Partisan in a fur jacket: Is that your own greatcoat or is it army
issue?

André (*hesitating*): I was issued it.

Partisan in a fur jacket: And your boots?

André: Boots, too.

Comrade in a fur jacket: They look like officer's boots to me.
He's lying.

Mykesha's Friend: Excuse me. What have you done with your
epaulettes?

André: I didn't have any.

Mykesha's Friend: This is a stupid conspiracy. Maybe you're a
captain or even higher in rank? Boys, what shall we do
with this counter-revolutionary?

Sailor: I'll tell you! (*To André*) You say that you are Andrew,
an officer-cadet in the reserve, forcibly called up. You say
you escaped. Why didn't you come to join the revolution?
Why didn't you do what poor Vania Makha did—he
refused to join the counter-revolution and said he would
rather die than go? And they killed him. I can't say any
more because my heart is too full. Who else wants to
speak?

Partisan in a fur cap: I suggest we do with him what they did with Vania.

Mykesha (*to Andrė*): Show me your hands. (*Looking at them*) No callouses. I vote for that too!

Partisan in a fur jacket (*testing the material of Andrė's greatcoat*): So do I!

Mykesha's Friend: I'm for his demobilization (*Waits to see the impact of his words.*) Take off the greatcoat and boots and put a red stamp on his forehead. (*He raises his rifle. The partisans make way.*)

Sailor: Don't touch him yet! Let's vote—who is for his death? (*Counts the votes.*) Who is for life? No one.

Andrė: Wait, comrades, I joined them to bring them harm.

The Whole Tribunal: Ho-ho! A real comedian.

Andrė: I was sent to them.

Fate: Who sent you?

Andrė hesitates.

Partisan with a fur cap: God sent him?

Andrė: A secret revolutionary group.

Fate: Which one? Have you a witness?

I (*stepping forward*): I'm a witness. I can vouch that he was mobilized and sent by us to the officer-cadets HQ. He was to report to us on their plans, quantities of arms and so on.

Fate: Who sent him from your side?

I: The local secret revolutionary HQ.

Fate: And who are you?

I give him the package. He reads:

"Comrade Fate. I am sending comrade Yuha to be your liaison. The workers' detachments have expelled the enemy from his position and are pursuing him. . .Hamar." (*To his men*) Let him go!

26

Andrė and I are walking in the corridor. Near Maryna's door I turn to him:

Please go in here!

27

André enters. He is met by Maryna.

Maryna: Are you free?

André: It's a miracle! Help came just in time. I am turning my back on the past and I'm beginning a new life. A new life!

Maryna: Psst! (*Ironically*) Don't be so loud! (*André meets his father in silence.*)

28

I walk downstairs. I feel cold and stop near the fire. A guard is warming himself at it. I stretch my hands to the fire.

First Guard: It's difficult to believe—revolution and battle all around us, but the fleas are still biting us.

Second Guard: It's night now, that's why they're biting.

Third Guard: I can hear a cock crowing.

First Guard (*with disbelief*): In the city?

Third Guard: Can you hear it?

I listen. Indeed, somewhere behind a wall I can hear the early legato *of a hoarse cock. The ill-fated call is heard three times. I recall the biblical myth about the apostle Peter when he betrayed Christ three times. I shudder and walk away.*

29

Georges is running capless. Suddenly he comes up against the guards.

Guard: Halt! (*Georges freezes like a statue of fear.*) Where are you going?

Georges: There.
Guard: Who are you?
Georges: I am Georges.
Guard: Do you live here?
Georges: No, I swear I don't. My sister lives here.
Guard: Who is your sister?
Georges: Zinka. She lives in the attic.
Guard: Who is she?
Georges: She's a prostitute.
> *He walks upstairs, followed by one of the guards who sees him to Zinka's door.*

30

Georges (*knocking*): Zinka!
Zinka: Who is it? (*She opens the door.*)
Georges: It's me. (*He goes in.*)
Zinka: Has your father sent you again? Get out!
Georges: No, I came on my own. Only for a second. I had a big surprise downstairs—the whole regiment of partisans. But I managed to fool them. I wasn't afraid of them. You don't believe me? No? Today I killed one of them. You know how it happened? He ran from behind a corner straight into me. My gun fired and he fell. Have you got some candy? Just a little? By the way, the sign blew off the sweetshop. The wind tore it off. Later the wind dropped. Guns were firing. Why are you looking at me like that?
Zinka: Why did you come? To hide?
Georges: Me? No! I don't want to hide. Only don't tell anyone that I'm here. By the way, I told them you were my sister.
Zinka: You've found a fine sister.
Georges: I wasn't serious, but I had to. You know I don't have a sister. Look how the moon is shining. By the way, I saw no blood. Everything was so strange and unpleasant. If only my mother were alive. I should pray to God, shouldn't I?
Zinka: Go on, pray!
Georges: God and my dear mother! Don't let Zinka betray me! (*He turns to her.*) You won't betray me? (*Knocking at the door*) Don't open! I implore you. (*He kneels in front of*

Zinka.) I promise I won't fight any more. I'm scared!

Zinka: But will you fire from the rooftop?

Georges: That's something quite different.

Zinka goes to open the door. Georges clings to the hem of her dress.

Georges: You are the Virgin Mary! You are my mother. Don't!

Zinka (*struck by the word "mother"*): Say that again, will you?

Georges: My mother.

Zinka: Mother. Then you are my child. Don't cry! If you like I'll give you my breast to suck. No! . . . What kind of a mother am I. . . .(*Angrily*) Be quiet! (*She opens the door.*)

31

Fate (*silently surveying the whole room, including the small window*): I can see at once where I am.

Zinka: Where?

Fate: They say you offer yourself to the bourgeois class.

Zinka: And what can your proletarian class offer me? You'll have to take your pants down like everyone else.

Fate: This isn't the point.

Zinka: So why did you come?

Fate: Did you see the legs? One of our men was half-buried, stuck in the ground like a cigarette butt. And now the general has escaped from our clutches. (*He sits down in disappointment.*)

Zinka (*offers Georges a candy*): Here, take it. You asked for it.

Fate: He ran away from Fate!

Zinka: Here, take his son.

Sailor (*looking closely*): He's too young. Where is your father?

Georges: I don't know.

Sailor: And does your father know where you are?

Georges: No, he doesn't.

Sailor: This is a real problem. (*He begins to ponder.*)

32

Stupay and Perotsky, each separately, are walking up and down the room. A shadow falls in the doorway to the second room. Maryna is sitting down. André's shadow moves restlessly. Stupay and old Perotsky walk quietly— they come together and whisper:

Perotsky: That's what comes of your Austrian idea of an autonomous Ukraine!

Stupay: It's the fault of your united Russia.

Perotsky: Independent!

Stupay: Indivisible!

They come together and almost fight. Just then the rattle of firearms is heard (Fate is escorting Georges), and they calm down and part. They come together again and again they part. Perotsky goes up to the window, lifts the tapestry a little and suddenly, as if struck by the cold rays of the moon, he shouts:

Fate is taking Georges somewhere. Oh my God! André! Well, I'll run myself! (*He runs downstairs, automatically shouting military orders.*) Halt!

André goes up to the window and suddenly puts his hand across his eyes. He moves back. Maryna comes up to him and says:

Turn your back on the past. Or else they will kill you and us. Your mistake was that you tried to foment a "Russian movement" in Ukraine. Now you must correct this mistake.

André: What is happening there in the street?

Maryna: A Bolshevik revolution. We must counteract it. You must go immediately to the neighboring villages. There are people there who have arms. I will write you a message.

André: What's happening down below?

Maryna: Down below? (*She looks through the window and is deeply shocked by what she sees. André is motionless. They are both waiting for the salvo. At last Maryna moves.*) They lowered the rifle and took him away. (*She writes.*) "To the brothers Zakrutenkos, Chornoyar village, to Dmytro Kopytsia in Buhaivka. I am sending you Ensign Perotsky on the orders of the committee of the golden mace. . . ."

André: Let's drop this mace, Marine! Let's drop everything and escape together to some green haven.

Maryna (*writing*): "Assist him immediately to gather partisan detachments, armed and mounted."

André: Is all this happening because I made the mistake of loving you?

Maryna (*signing the message*): "Member of the committee, Seagull." (*To André*) The password is "the pipe is lit." That's all. Go!

ACT FIVE

1

Once more, imagine, my friends, a street lined with fragrant acacias. A red flag flies on the balcony of the Perotskys' apartment. It is sunny. Nastia is sitting down and embroidering in gold another flag. Beside her Zinka is singing:

> A maiden sits on the shore
> Embroidering a silk kerchief. . . .

Enter Luka.

Luka: How is your flag doing?

Nastia: Look! (*She unfolds it.*)

Luka: Is it ready, then?

Nastia: It will be finished in an hour.

Luka (*reading with great relish*): "Proletarians of All Countries Unite." Hammer and sickle. "Ukrainian Socialist Soviet Republic." (*Enthusiastically*) We've won! Wonderful! It's a pity Ilko isn't here to see it. He used to vacillate between some vision and love. (*To Zinka*) How are you, comrade Zinka?

Zinka: Could you give me some work now?

Luka: We shall! There'll be plenty of work. Not during the first stage of the revolution when fighting and destruction are going on. But after that there'll be work. As soon as reconstruction begins we'll even be able to think of love. Because love is not an escape and a dream, as it was with Ilko, but a function. (*He flexes the muscles of his arm.*) Yes, a function! That reminds me, I have a meeting where I am to talk about the new functions of my sub-sections. So you say that the flag will be ready in an hour. I'll be back by then.

90

Zinka: Wait, you said that Ilko's love was a dream. What kind of a dream?

Luka: She just plays the piano, and he made a dream out of her.

Zinka: So that's who she is? Have you ever seen her up close?

Luka: No! I'll come back. (*He runs off.*)

Zinka: I must have a good look at that dream. (*She begins to sing a song.*)

2

Maryna, with her face pressed against the window. Stupay is telling fortunes stealthily by opening and shutting the Bible.

Maryna (*with great emotion*): Just a moment, father! Come here! To the window! A man passed on the other side with a pipe in his mouth. Come here and see if he comes back. I'll run to the dining room window. You can see more from there. (*She runs out.*)

Stupay (*after standing for a while at the window, goes back*): So she is playing Nat Pinkerton. I'll tell the future for the last time. Not from the Bible, from the *Kobzar.** What will be, will be. For the last time! (*Takes out the Kobzar and removes blue and yellow bookmarks from it. Puts the book on the table. Then solemnly places three fingers on the book.*) Will there or won't there be a Ukraine?

Maryna (*from the doorway*): Are you looking out, father?

Stupay: Of course! (*After a pause, to himself*) First column, line thirty three. (*He opens the book and finds the place.*) "The Cossacks will not come back, the Hetmans will not rise, Ukraine will not be covered by military tunics." (*Bitterly shaking his head*) Have I made a mistake? Or perhaps they are running away from the steppes? With their spears bent like crosses? No! Once more, this time for the last time. Second column, line seven.

---

*A book of poems by the Ukrainian poet, Taras Shevchenko, who is revered as a national prophet.

91

Maryna: Can you see, father? It may be him.

Stupay: Don't interrupt, Maryna! (*Opens and reads*) "You will perish, Ukraine, and be lost without a trace. . . ." (*In deep fright*) So for the third and last time. Will there or won't there be? . . .

3

Maryna (*from the threshold of the other room*): There will be!

Stupay (*angry*): Don't joke!

Maryna: Yes, there will be, my gray fortune teller.

Stupay: So you have become a Pythia, too?

Maryna: If you say so, yes! Ancient writers said that Pythia was a very beautiful girl in the beginning. She sat in a temple on the stone Omphalos, which means the center of the earth. There was an inscription on the gate: "Know thyself." So I shall now invoke it: "Ukrainian, know thyself." (*She is overcome by an extraordinary rapture. To her father*) Come to the window and stand there so that you won't be seen from the street.

Stupay: What's all this for?

Maryna (*behaving like Pythia*): The first thing you see will give you an answer as to whether there'll be a Ukraine. On this side, next to the wall, a man is standing.

Stupay (*humorously*): Well, what of it?

Maryna: Look at him. (*She plays a few chords from the* Sonata Pathetique.)

Stupay: He lit his pipe and went away. He pushed his hat to the back of his head. Is he your hero?

Maryna: Yes, he is. That is our password: "The pipe is lit." The pipe of counter-revolution. Today! (*She rapturously plays some chords from the* Sonata Pathetique.) Do you hear, father? Do you hear, my gray mustache, how our Cossacks are racing from the neighboring villages? We are ready! (*She gets up as if in ecstasy.*) Omphalos, omphalos! The pipes have been lit! (*She dances.*) No matter how strong the wind from the north it won't blow out the fire. No, it will intensify it. Blow until the sparks fly! (*She strikes the*

92

keyboard.) Omphalos! Light your pipes so that the smoke spreads across the steppe and into the heavens. Smoke until the sky is dense with it, until God sends you an angel who, as in a folktale, will ask you: "What do you want, you Cossacks, who have smoked so much?" We want our own state under this flag. (*With her hair streaming across her back she brings out the flag she has been hiding and unfolds it.*) Under this flag!

Stupay (*enchanted by the flag*): When did you embroider it? (*Knocking at the door.*)

Maryna (*rolls the flag; composed*): Come in!

4

Zinka (*holding a flag*): You don't have any thread, do you? I need it to finish embroidering the last letter. (*She unfolds the flag.*) If you have, may I borrow it? (*She gazes at Maryna.*)

Stupay: Well, well, the inscription is in Ukrainian. (*Reading*) "Proletarians of all Countries Unite." Hammer and sickle. And what does USSR stand for?

Zinka: Ukrainian Socialist Soviet Republic. They say this is the new national emblem.

Stupay: Whose flag is it?

Zinka: It's from the revolutionary HQ. I have to have it finished in an hour.

Stupay (*reading the inscription again*): Without a single mistake. (*He looks at Maryna.*)

Maryna: Not a single one.

Zinka (*looking closer at Maryna*): I thought you had blue eyes. You must look well in yellow.

Maryna: I thought yours were hazel, but they are bloodshot.

Zinka: I haven't slept for three nights, that's why my eyes are red. I've been embroidering the red banner—perhaps that's why my eyes are red and yours are blue. (*She leaves.*)

Stupay: Perhaps we have some?

Maryna: What?

Stupay: Thread.

Maryna: You are funny, father. You can't embroider an independent Ukraine with Russian red bunting.

Stupay: It's a pity we're like orphans.

5

*I walk upstairs to the revolutionary HQ. Zinka passes me
by. Maryna steps out of the doorway. For one second we
stop, look at each other and part.*

Zinka: So she's your dream? I thought she must be something
special, but she's just an ordinary girl in a skirt. Good
morning, neighbor!

I (*not understanding what Zinka is talking about*): Good
morning!

6

Stupay alone:

This is a flag and that is a flag. I am thinking of making the
following proposal: on the yellow and blue background
the lettering should be "Long Live Soviet Ukraine." Let it
be socialist, if only it's a Ukrainian republic. Or else: on
the red background two stripes, yellow and blue. . . .
(*Thinking*)

7

*Imagine the revolutionary HQ in the Perotsky apartment.
The scene resembles a bivouac. Men in greatcoats, with and
without rifles. A Red guard is sleeping. A line of
petitioners can be seen. People are constantly coming and
going. Hamar, the member of HQ, is busy. He sits next to
the telephone, and Luka and I are taking down his orders.
Behind him a workman is laying a telephone cable. On the
other side of the partition Ovram is sitting on a sofa.*

Hamar (*telephoning*): I'm coming at once! (*To Luka*) Something's odd. The Slobidsky HQ wants me to come over immediately. Some urgent matter which they don't want to discuss on the phone. Take my place while I'm gone. (*Before leaving*) Send a telegram to all revolutionary committees in the villages: "First task—sow more wheat." (*With a wide sweep of the hand*) The steppes!

Luka: Where's the seed?

Hamar: Buried in the ground on the farms. (*He leaves.*)

A voice in the doorway: Can you tell us, please, where the Bolshevik movement is?

Ovram (*at the switchboard*): What is your business?

Voices: We walk upon the soil, but we don't own any.

Ovram: I'm connecting you.

Luka (*shouting at those at the door*): All those without any land step forward! (*To me*) Cable "Second: Organize the poor peasants. Tell the rich peasants that their houses won't be their own much longer. Third: On that side of the Dnieper there are deposits of coke. . . ." Who is snoring over there?

Voices: Comrade, wake up. You'll sleep through the revolution.

Luka (*standing on the table*): Comrades! The revolutionary committee is not a bedroom. It isn't even a railway station where you can doze. It's a locomotive. . . .

New voices from the door: Comrade Luka, we've confiscated some arms. Seven rifles and three pistols. What should we do with them?

Luka: Take them to our supply depot.

A Voice: We've dug up some rugs and clothes.

Luka: Take them to the supply section.

Voice: Ten corsets.

Luka: Bury them. (*To me*) You should take a look at the schools and see which of them need repairs. (*To the worker*) No, that's not the way to do it. Let me. . . . (*He climbs the ladder and fixes the cable.*)

Ovram's voice: Switchboard! What! What cavalry? You must be dreaming. It's probably not horses but fleas jumping over you.

Luka (*climbing down, to me*) Secondly: we need to print Ukrainian primers. (*He notes something down.*) Who wants land? (*Takes notes, to me*) What about the teachers? (*To those at the door*) Come on up! (*He takes notes and looks at his watch.*)

Ovram (*in a different, alarmed voice*): They have chevrons? One moment!

Luka (*to me*): You must find out those teachers who know Ukrainian. (*To the line-up*) Who's first?

An alarmed voice at the door: Comrades! Some bandits are attacking us. Cavalry with chevrons! (*Artillery fire is heard in the distance as if to confirm this.*)

Luka: Who's first in line? I bet some bourgeois. . . .

Ovram's voice: I'll connect you (*the telephone crackles*).

Luka: (*into the receiver*) Hamar isn't here. You asked him to come over—you didn't? (*He sways a little.*) Don't panic! What? The bells are ringing in the monastery? What? Cavalry? Stop them. I'm dispatching a detachment to help you. (*To those in the doorway*) Where are the arms you dug up?

Voice: They're here.

Luka: Bring them here. (*He climbs onto the table and addresses everyone.*) Comrades! Do you hear that those first in line were bourgeois? What do they want? They want to block our road to socialism. Those who want to help us must first line up for arms. They must fight! Who's first?
Some come up. I try to stand second in line, but someone in a greatcoat pushes me aside. At last, fifth in the row, I get a rifle. Some men line up unwillingly and some sneak out and flee.

Luka: Fall in! (*We fall in.*)

Ovram: Only those who have legs can fall in. Anyone who's without them has to crawl.

Luka: How's the telephone?

Ovram: It doesn't work.

Luka: That means someone's cut it off. Comrades! Our class enemies are pressing us from all sides. Our goal is socialism. By the left, quick march!
(*We follow Luka downstairs into the street.*)

8

Stupay alone:

For the third and last time. Do you hear, Taras? What kind of Ukraine will it be? (*Artillery salvo; Stupay in desperation*) They won't let me finish my fortune-telling. (*He opens the book and reads.*) "Bury me and then rise up." (*He runs away, capless, holding the book high in his hand.*)

9

Stupay comes out into the street. He sees Ovram crawling. Otherwise the street is empty. From the distance he hears desultory firing. Stupay stands at the crossroads hesitating:

Well, I've risen. But I don't know which side I should join. (*He thinks and hesitates.*) Neither this side nor that. (*The bullets whizz by.*) Wait. There are Ukrainians on both sides. What are you doing? Let me think! They're firing at each other; glad that they have ammunition. (*Deliberates*) I'll join the red banner. The Zaporozhians had a red flag too. The dumy* say that dead Zaporozhians were covered with a red banner. But then, Kulish** writes that the Zaporozhians had white banners with red crosses on them. I can join the yellow and blue colors—but these aren't Zaporozhian. I suggested red, yellow and blue stripes, but they won't listen to me. (*A flower, cut by a bullet, falls to the ground. Stupay picks it up.*) So they'll destroy all the flowers, will kill mother earth, the wheat, the sunflowers— what are you doing? (*A bullet strikes him in the chest.*) So there you are. (*He falls.*)

---

*Ukrainian epic folk songs, originating in the 17th century.
**Panteleimon Kulish (1819-97), a Ukrainian writer.

Ovram (*crawls near*): How are you, neighbor?

Stupay (*trying to smile*): It's interesting. . . .

Ovram: What is?

Stupay: The bullet—which side did it come from?

Ovram (*tearing off a piece of kerchief*): The main thing is you weren't hit in the legs. . . . (*He tries to bind the wound but realizes that Stupay is dying. Several Red guards run by. One of them calls out "Someone is attacking our rear! Run!"*)

Ovram: You can't run away from death. Stand still!

Stupay hears the last words and tries to repeat them, but can't. With a last effort he raises his hand. The world is a blur for him encompassing the sky and the steppe. The fleeing Red guards step over Stupay, but he thinks they are the old Zaporozhians on horses. Music is heard (from the allegro molto*). It's enchanting. Only the sun is burning his chest. Soon it sets. He feels better, but it is dark everywhere and the music is barely audible.*

10

Nationalist partisans come running up. Ovram is sitting still. Stupay is dying. Andrè has stopped nearby. He shouts: "A stretcher!" They bring a stretcher. Andrè, pointing to Ovram, tells them to pick him up.

A Partisan (*to Ovram*): Come on, get up!

Ovram: That's impossible.

11

The red flag falls from Perotsky's balcony. No one knows who knocked it down. In its place there appears a yellow and blue flag. No one knows who put it there.

12

Maryna, with a bouquet of flowers, goes to meet André. Hearing the bells:

It's just like Easter. They say that in the monastery you praised the northern star. Does that mean Russia?

André (*seriously and firmly*): Yes.

Maryna: Why did you keep silent about Ukraine?

André: We won't talk about that.

Maryna (*looking sharply into his eyes*): What about Ukraine?

André: Here is a corpse. (*He gently steers her away from Stupay's body.*) Don't dirty yourself. (*They both recognize Stupay.*)

Maryna: Father! (*She cannot believe he's dead.*) You.... (*Realizing that he is dead she kneels and kisses his hand.*) You are funny, father. (*She puts down his hand and stammers some incoherent words.*) My father, his grizzled mustache, his gray tuft of hair!

13

The yellow and blue flag falls quietly down from Perotsky's balcony. No one knows who knocked it down. An Imperial Russian tricolor appears in its place. No one knows who put it up.

ACT SIX

1

The street where the Perotskys live is alive with people. A crowd gathers outside the house. Festive atmosphere, exchange of greetings, mostly by ladies carrying parasols. Solemn ringing of bells can be heard from the churches.

First Lady: Varvara Mykhailivna, how are you, dear?

Second Lady: You should greet me with "Christ is Risen."

First Lady: Only now do I realize how glad he must have been to have risen.

The husband of the second lady (*Zinka's visitor*): Still, Christ was tortured by people, not by Bolshevik beasts.

First Lady: The last three days I spent as if I were in a grave.

Second Lady: My dear, I was a corpse, too. . . .

The husband of the first lady (*also Zinka's visitor*): Yes, they drove us into the cellars. They wanted to make corpses out of us and graves out of our houses. It's very odd that they are going to be tried like normal people.

Second Lady: They are going to try them?

Zinka's Visitor: Imagine, they'll try them before they execute them.

Professor: Liberalism all over again!

2

Ovram is carried by four stretcher-bearers. Seeing the crowd he orders them:

100

Quick march, stretcher-bearers. I am being paraded. One-two! Left-right! Sing! If you don't want to sing, I will myself. (*He sings a refrain from a well-known military song.*) Attention! Bourgeois—eyes left! Salute the proletariat!

Voices: What cynicism! What effrontery!

Ovram: Now put me on a throne!

Voices: How dare he! Shut his mouth! (*A lady tries to poke him in the eyes with her parasol, but misses.*)

Ovram: You're a real flirt! (*A second lady is trying to hit him.*) Off with you, black crows. I'm not dead yet. Put your parasols away—they won't shield you from the storm of the revolution.

3

Ovram is carried into a room—in front of the court. The presiding judge is making a public speech:

Gentlemen, today we are trying a secret Chekist.* He tried us in cellars, at night, with no witnesses. We are bringing him into the daylight in front of your eyes. This is a public trial. Moreover, while we are putting Bolshevism on trial, we are giving it an opportunity to defend its bloody doctrines in public. Furthermore, we are offering to everyone in this hall an opportunity to speak for or against this criminal. The statue of Themis, the symbol of justice which was buried by the Bolsheviks, is now restored to its position on this table. (*To Ovram*) Accused, what is your name?

Ovram: Ovram or Yakiv, it's all the same. It's not the name you are going to execute.

Judge: What was your profession before you joined the Cheka?

Ovram: I crawled upon the earth on which you walk.

Judge: What did you do in the Cheka?

Ovram: What do you think?

*Member of the Bolshevik secret police—the Cheka.

Judge: How old are you?

Ovram: I'm thirty and I won't live much longer.

Judge: Are you a Bolshevik?

Ovram: Half of me.

Judge: That means? (*Ovram shows his truncated body*.) The legs don't matter. You are a Bolshevik. Now tell us why you haven't retreated with the Bolsheviks, but have remained behind?

Ovram: If my legs don't matter, then your question doesn't matter either.

Judge: You want to blame your legs?

Ovram: I should blame your heads, not my legs.

Judge: What's that?

Ovram: If you hadn't started the war, I would still have my legs and would have retreated with the Bolsheviks.

Voices: What effrontery! A cynic!

Judge: But we know that you were left here for a purpose, to spy on us. What do you say to that?

Ovram: What other work can I find while you're in power?

Judge: Witness General Perotsky. (*Perotsky stands up*.) Your excellency, please speak.

Perotsky: It was through this window that I saw the prisoner and the fellow with one eye. The legless man showed them where I live and probably where Georges was hiding too. I stood near the window and saw the man with one eye lead Georges away. Gentlemen, my boy was crying. He was trying to kiss the man's hand, but he was pushed away. I couldn't watch it any longer. I shouted a word of command: halt. And he dared to raise his rifle against me. But he was stopped by the others, and they took me to their HQ.

Judge: What did you see there?

Perotsky: It was a nightmare. At night a monk joined me in my cell and he prayed the whole night—in Ukrainian. Imagine that! I couldn't sleep. It was this monk who told me that the legless man hammers nails into epaulettes and is quite well paid for it.

Judge: Did you hammer nails into epaulettes?

Ovram: I'd rather hammer them into your heads.

Judge: You informed on Georges. How did you do that?

Zinka pops out of the audience:

I'll tell you. I'm a witness (*pointing to Ovram*) against him.

So help me God! Just let me! (*The court makes no decision, but she carries on.*) To inform on Georges, that innocent angel, was a very serious crime. How could he (*pointing to Ovram*) do it? Georges was such a nice boy. He loved to eat chocolate, pray to God and shoot pigeons. Remember how he once fired at a pigeon from the roof? Too bad he missed the pigeon and hit a man.(*Approval in the hall.*)

Judge: Please come closer to the table.

Zinka: Georges came to me from the front. He had killed a Bolshevik and was being followed. He asked me to hide him and tell the partisans he was my brother. My heart bled for him. Then the partisan with one eye missing came in. He searched for the general and was very worried in case he'd fled. Then I gave Georges some candy and I said to the partisan: take his son. (*A storm breaks out in the hall. Judge gives orders to have Zinka removed.*)

Judge (*to Ovram*): You will be forgiven if you tell us which Bolsheviks stayed in the town. (*Ovram remains silent.*) No? Then take him out and shoot him! (*On the stairs Ovram stops his guards.*)

Ovram: Stop! I'll say something. (*The guard stops.*) But before I say it I want to smoke. I'll tell you for one cigarette. (*He is given a cigarette. He lights it and draws on it. Puts on his cap.*) Go on, carry me!

ACT SEVEN

1

Again at the Perotskys. It's night. Luka at the telephone.

Luka: HQ? Comrade Hamar? This is Luka. The bandits have been crushed. The town is in our hands. I've found some interesting documents. André Perotsky's raid was supported, it appears, by some local secret organization. How many casualties? Quite a few. Yes, I hear you. I understand. . . .

2

I come back from the battlefront. I meet Luka. A feeling of joy and exaltation. Indeed, a memorable meeting.

Luka: Hallo there!

I: How are you, brother?

Luka: Where were you after the battle? Were you gazing at the stars?

I: I was putting out old stars and lighting new ones.

Luka: Now, that victory is ours? Do you know who organized and led that raid? Perotsky. We found a letter on the body of a dead counter-revolutionary. Here it is. (*He reads.*) "To Chornoyar village, to Dmytro Kopytsia in Buhaivka. I am sending you Ensign Perotsky on the orders of the committee of the golden mace. . . . Assist him immediately to gather partisan detachments, armed and mounted." It is

104

signed by a "member of the committee, Seagull." Now we know why there were so many casualties. Did you know that your neighbor Zinka was tortured to death and Ovram was executed outside the town, near a garbage dump? They said that he. . . .

Something soundless and dark is approaching me. The candle is flickering. Luka's voice, in the distance, sounds to me like a death warrant.

I: Luka, I always. . . .

Luka: What?

I: The candle isn't steady.

Luka: The candle?

I: It's half-burned.

Luka: They say that he said, "Thank you for the funeral. I would give you some money for tea but I have none. Never mind, the proletarian class will pay you back." They say that Nastia lost her mind when she heard the news. Well, are you coming?

I: No! I mean yes, I'll go.

Luka: To your place?

I: Yes, to my place. . . .

3

I walk up the staircase, unconsciously and automatically. Where to? I must go to my place. I must find the time to go to my place and search my own soul. I must talk to myself about treason and about death. First about treason. I recall the details of my treason. Suddenly I see that I am outside Stupay's door. It is half-closed. I hear snoring. I peep in. A hoarse voice asks "Who is it?"

I: Tell me please. The Stupays lived here. . . .

Voice: A girl. She's in the basement now. This is signals HQ.

*At last, my friends, a finale. I am outside the door in the
basement. I listen. My sense of hearing is so acute now that
I can hear time and the stars in outer space. I hear a drop
of water falling behind the door. But I cannot hear anyone
stirring. Is she asleep? I knock and the door opens. She
stands there holding a candle.*

She: It's you?

I: It's me.

She: By the knocking I could tell that someone was coming
who was different from those upstairs, someone quiet,
someone very close. . . .

I: Yes, someone has come. Someone, who, alas, is different
from those upstairs, who is not close to anyone.

She: A poet came with an open heart. I'm so happy. I was
waiting for you. Forgive me for not coming out to meet
you. But I no longer have my room (*pointing upstairs*). It's
not my fault. It was taken away from me.

I: It doesn't matter. You and I will soon find a room of our
own.

She: That's a hint at your poet's attic? (*She raises her left
eyebrow.*) Thank you. But right here, while I was waiting
for you, I planted a garden of love. Can you see it? The
marble steps. Beautiful, aren't they? There (*pointing to the
water leaking*) is a fountain and water-clock, all in one.
When you spend the night here you hear the drumbeat of
eternity. . . .

I: They say that a worker lived here with his wife. He was at the
front, and she counted the drops day and night. . . .

She (*restlessly*): Yes. But here (*pointing to the bench*) is a
garden bench. Especially reserved for poets. Sit down, my
dear guest. You must be tired. No? I don't know how to
receive you. I would play for you, but they've separated
me from my piano. What good is it to them? Who, on their
side, can play? Tell me, who will play the piano?

I: Don't worry, they'll play.

She: Will they play the *Pathetique*?

I: First of all.

She: You think so? (*Pensively*) How I should like to play it now. The sonata about the youth racing on a horse in the steppes, asking the winds where to go. Do you remember Easter night? (*She moves her hands as if on a keyboard.*) I was writing a letter to you then. Do you want me to show it to you? I saved it. How long I had waited for you. (*Her left hand as if on a keyboard, the right hand as if writing*) I saw you in my dreams; in the distant blue ages I flew to you.

*I begin to hear music (*rondo*). What is this? My nerves? Hallucinations? Hypnosis? I must bring this to an end. It's high time!*

I: Tell me, did you fly like a seagull?

She (*with her hands at her sides; confused as a little girl not knowing what to say*): No! No! I just flew. . . .

I: Like a gnat?

She (*straightens up, feeling instinctively that she has made a bad impression*): No! No! (*Defiantly*) Yes! I flew like a seagull. (*Conquering her indecision*) Tell me, have you come to write verses about the seagull or to take her away?

I: I came to ask her simply, without any allegories. Tell me, would you like to come with me upstairs and tell them our stories?

She: What about?

I: What about? For instance, about the legless worker who lived in the basement, the poet who lived in the attic and a girl who lived for music. How the girl deceived the poet, began to play with a golden mace, how she, with the help of the poet, brought in the officers, how they carried the legless man and killed him? I'm going to tell them that I am a traitor, and you will tell them that you are the Seagull.

She: So they don't know yet?

I: If they knew they would come to fetch us. They would remind us that he alone will be victorious who is prepared to carry his ideas to the scaffold and declare them in the face of death. Are you ready?

She (*confused as a little girl, her hands clutching an apron*): I?

I: Ovram carried his ideas to his death. So did Zinka. Are you going to carry them to the table upstairs? Will you tell them?

She (*her hands are off the apron*): Yes, I'll tell them. (*She begins to clutch the apron again.*) Perhaps I'd better tell you.

I: Then I will report you. Will you let me do this?

She (*under control*): If you do that your punishment will be reduced.

I: That isn't the point. As soon as I had helped to liberate André Perotsky I walked the whole night through the steppes. That was my first monologue about treason and death. I concluded that it wouldn't be enough of a punishment if I killed myself. I was ready to accept whatever Luka, society and the working class gave me. I would have gone and told them. But I didn't go because I carried in my heart your shining image, because I didn't know that your bright eyes hid a cold, black conspiracy.

She (*defiantly*): I'll tell them myself. I'll tell them that I am the Seagull. I'll say: I am that seagull which flew over Zhovti Vody, over the wide bypaths of Ukraine, which still lives in every Cossack heart. I'll say.... (*She begins to waver again.*) Perhaps I should change before I go?

I: Go as you are.

She: No, I'd better change. Just a moment. Tell me what to put on.

I: You should wear an armor of bravery.

She: Wait, one moment. I'll go as I am.

I: Let's go!

She: Let's. (*She follows me.*) You see I was in love with you and still am. I'm telling you this quite openly. (*She stops on the threshold.*) Perhaps we shouldn't go. Instead, let's go away from here, far away, and let's give up everything except our lives. Darling, let's go and simply live somewhere. In a house with a well outside. I would come out carrying empty pails, and you would be at the well. I would take you into the wide rye fields. (*She makes movements with her hands, as if spreading apart the rye and taking me with her.*) Cornflowers and white birches dot the field. Can you see? Can you smell the scent of love?

I (*walking upstairs, grumbling*): You still repeat the old sentimental songs.

She (*behind me*): You see, I tried to smother my first love, and now it is crying. Wait a moment, I'll try to quieten it. Quiet, my love. I'll buy you a Ukrainian reed-pipe and I'll sing to you:

Rocka-bye, baby,
Silken strands,
Golden reeds,
Silver bells,
You're safe in your cradle,
Sleep well, my baby!

(*I take her by the hand.*) Where are you taking me? To the torturers? No, let me go. I cannot. . . .

I (*letting her hand fall; trying to persuade myself rather than her*): You see, someone else who prayed and suffered lived here.

She: Who will tell my old mother how I went to church for the passion, how I carried a candle home (*she pretends to carry a candle*) and you, the lusty wind (*she shields her imaginary candle from me and goes down*), want to blow out the candle of my life.

I (*feeling that in a moment I'll give in to her*): Luka! (*I shout.*) Luka! (*Seeing Luka on the stairs I gather strength. I seize her hand and take her up to Luka.*) Here is my dream: The Seagull. . . .

She: No!

I: Yes! Do you remember the first uprising? The wind, the moon? Then Ensign Perotsky fell into comrade Fate's hands. Fate didn't know who he was, although he felt instinctively he was an enemy and wanted to do away with him. But I intervened. I was sent by Hamar, but she saw me on the stairs and asked me to save André Perotsky. I saved him. She was my dream and for two years I raced after that vision through the steppes, although she lived a few yards away from me. Then she asked me to save the man who was our enemy. How could I not show kindness and love? I was detached from the masses, lost somewhere in the attic between heaven and earth. My thoughts were the cobweb of a dreamer who thought he could reconcile heaven and earth. I was a dreamer who wanted to find a bridge between the ideal and the mob, between the nation and its future. The result is familiar: the ruin and death of comrades, a dead interval in the revolutionary struggle. I am the author of that interval, Luka!

Luka: Tell me one thing: did you know that she was the Seagull.

I: No!

She: He knew it—I told him. . . .

Luka (*giving orders to the red guards to take Maryna away; after waiting till they had escorted her away, again turning to me*) Tell me, as a friend, did you know?

I: No, I didn't. But I knew who Perotsky was.

Luka (*deep in thought, speaking more to himself*): Well, the raid would have taken place even without Perotsky. But you freed Perotsky and that is treason.

I: Yes, I admit it's treason, Luka. As long as I live its shadow will follow me.

Luka: True, it was not intentional. It has passed, it was the result of your attic dreams. (*Turning to me*) You must learn a lesson from it. There are many temptations waiting for us on our way to our distant goal. Now go. I'll lock you up, and tomorrow you'll face the revolutionary tribunal. You must be tried. But I am your friend. Have you eaten yet today? (*He takes me into Perotsky's room. We shake hands. Luka leaves and closes the door. I hear his words.*) Good night, Ilko!

I: No, good morning, Luka. See, it's dawn. . . .

I feel relieved. The window flashes like a fiery banner. I feel an extraordinary exaltation. I can hear the cosmos playing a symphony pathetique, first on helicons and trombones, then on clarinets, flutes and violins. I know that at this moment Luka is looking through the window too and hearing this symphony.